Shel Silverstein

Twayne's United States Authors Series

Ruth K. MacDonald, Editor

TUSAS 688

((*Shel Silverstein*))

Ruth K. MacDonald

Twayne Publishers

New York

For Cameron, my guinea pig, and Lee, my gerbil

Twayne's United States Authors Series No. 688

Shel Silverstein
Ruth K. MacDonald

Twayne Publishers

1633 Broadway
New York, NY 10019

Library of Congress Cataloging-in-Publication Data

MacDonald, Ruth K.
  Shel Silverstein / Ruth K. MacDonald.
    p. cm. — (Twayne's United States authors series ; TUSAS 688)
  Includes bibliographical references and index.
  ISBN 0-8057-1606-8 (alk. paper)
  1. Silverstein, Shel—Criticism and interpretation. I. Title.
II. Series.
PS3569.I47224Z77   1997
811'.54—dc21
                                                    97-15204
                                                    CIP

10 9 8 7 6 5

Printed in the United States of America

Contents

Preface

Shel Silverstein is admittedly not a great technical poet; he will not be remembered for the advances he has made in the rhyme, meter, diction, or form of his poetry, which children have come to love so much. What he has accomplished is bringing poetry—perhaps more accurately described as light verse—to children who would otherwise avoid it. His advances in the field of children's poetry are twofold: he has made his poetry popular enough to endure for the past 20 years or so and for the foreseeable future, and he has chosen to write about unusual topics.

The unmentionable gets mentioned in Silverstein's volumes, and the less savory, the decidedly unpastoral, and the unidyllic, areas from which children's poets have voluntarily banished themselves, are his playground and inspiration. In an age in which children are regularly confronted with divorce and death, not to mention racial and ethnic hatred, environmental degradation, and a general lack of culturally shared values, Silverstein's poetry both affirms the pleasures of life and gives voice and validity to the depression, boredom, and general uncooperativeness and loneliness of modern life for children. The two volumes of poetry that are the main concern of this study, *Where the Sidewalk Ends* and *The Light in the Attic,* are certainly period pieces. Like the works of the poets who preceded Silverstein, they were the leading edge of children's poetry in their time. Edward Lear's limericks, Robert Louis Stevenson's *Garden,* A. A. Milne's two volumes of verse about Christopher Robin and friends, and the works of Ogden Nash and John Ciardi were all trailblazers in their time, and yet those works, too, have begun to show their age. Like most of these earlier works, most of Silverstein's will eventually become outdated, but there are still a precious few poems, among his works and those of his predecessors, that will endure because they speak for children so precisely and without historical limitations.

This book examines the technical aspects of Silverstein's poetry only sparingly and only as it elucidates the effectiveness, or lack thereof, of an individual poem. Silverstein's poetry does not reward such technical examination, nor is technicality his strength. No amount of critical perspective makes the verse any better or the appeal to children any clearer; the approach here is thoroughly pragmatic.

The heart of this volume is in chapters 3 and 4, extended examinations of *Where the Sidewalk Ends* and *The Light in the Attic*. Had Silverstein not written these two volumes, there would be no need for a study such as this because he would have garnered neither the fame nor the place in children's literature that he has attained. My intent in these two chapters is to examine the experience of the books from a child reader's perspective, mediated by my own adult perspective and overlaid with a knowledge of the broader issues in poetry for both adults and children. These two chapters examine the various unities of the books: organization and design, theme, illustration. Selected poems in each volume, especially the least and most successful ones, receive full explication. The chapters also contain some discussion of the books' critical reception, at publication and since. My goal in both chapters is to determine why these books remain popular with children and to go beyond each book's surface appearance, beyond the simple cartoons and naughty jokes, to see what else informs and deepens the volumes' reading and viewing. My hope is that my comments make apparent the tacit perceptions of readers, both young and less young.

Silverstein, like many poets and authors, is an intensely private person, and I have respected his unwillingness to supply personal information to the public, especially in chapter 1, which presents such biographical information as can be obtained from various scholarly sources. Silverstein had a successful career as a *Playboy* cartoonist and published several minor volumes of cartoons and other photographically illustrated books through the Playboy press; these are dealt with summarily and primarily in this necessarily short chapter.

Chapter 2 deals with works that are designed for children on at least one level: *The Giving Tree* and *Lafcadio, the Lion Who Shot Back*, two longer works in prose, and a small group of picture books. All published before the poetry volumes, these works show Silverstein's talents in prose as well as in illustration and can be seen as his rehearsal of the use of symbols and allegory. The progress of the narratives in these books, and especially the lack of resolution or clear message in the two longer works' endings, introduce major themes about human relations and human self-definition in a social setting. They also show Silverstein's provoking and provocative method of inducing a reader's multiple interpretation of an allegory or parable. The issues involved in marketing these books for a popular audience, including their design and their persistence in print, are also discussed here, as is the critical reception of *Tree*.

Chapter 5 looks at two picture books published after the poetry volumes, both much less substantial in content but marketed and designed to build on the success of the poetry. The final chapter locates Silverstein in the tradition of children's poetry and discusses not only his predecessors but also his successors. It includes an extended discussion of the theories of children's humor and of Silverstein's successes as a humorist and as a poet. A discussion of *Falling Up*, Silverstein's late reappearance in children's poetry, fits here as the culmination of his career.

Acknowledgments

Selections from *Where the Sidewalk Ends* and *A Light in the Attic* are used by permission of HarperCollins Publishers.
No book is published without indebtedness to others. I owe a scholarly debt to Perry Nodelman's scholarship, without which this book would have remained isolated, unconnected rumination about illustration, poetry, and popular literature for children. Michael Pownall's expertise with three different computer programs during the seven years it took to write this book deserves more than thanks, as does his toleration for my preoccupation and distraction. My children get their just reward in the dedication.

Chronology

1932   Born 25 September in Chicago.

1950s Begins army service in Korea; contributes cartoon to *Pacific Stars and Stripes.*

1956   First cartoon published in *Playboy* magazine.

1960   *Now Here's My Plan: A Book of Futilities* is published.

1961   *Uncle Shelby's ABZ: A Primer for Tender Young Minds* is published.

1963   *A Playboy's Teevee Jeebies* and *Lafcadio, the Lion Who Shot Back* are published.

1964   *The Giving Tree, A Giraffe and a Half, Who Wants a Cheap Rhinoceros?,* and *Uncle Shelby's Zoo: Don't Bump the Glump!* are published.

1965   *A Playboy's Teevee Jeebies: Do It Yourself Dialogue for the Late Late Show* is published.

1968   Writes score for motion picture *Dirty Feet;* album *Drain My Brain* is released.

1970   Writes score for motion picture *Ned Kelly.*

1971   Appears in and writes the original score for the movie *Who Is Harry Kellerman and Why Is He Saying Those Terrible Things about Me?*

1972   The albums *Freakin' at the Freakers Ball, Sloppy Seconds,* and *Dr. Hook* are released.

1973   The album *Bobby Bare Sings Lullabys, Legends, and Lies: The Songs of Shel Silverstein* is released.

1974   *Where the Sidewalk Ends* is published; receives award for *New York Times* Outstanding Book.

1976   *The Missing Piece* is published.

1979   *Different Dances* is published.

1980   Writes score for motion picture *The Great Conch Train Robbery.*

1981   *A Light in the Attic* is published and chosen as one of *School Library Journal*'s Best Books for 1981; *The Missing Piece Meets the Big O* is published; receives the Michigan Young Readers' Award for *Sidewalk;* one-act play *The Lady or the Tiger* is performed at New York City Ensemble Studio Theatre.

1982   *Big O* is chosen one of the International Reading Association's Children's Choices; makes last contribution to *Playboy,* "The Twenty Commandments."

1983   *Attic* receives Buckeye Award.

1984   Records selections from *Attic* and *Sidewalk* for CBS records.

1996   *Falling Up* is published.

Chapter One

The Private Poet

Shel Silverstein, or more formally, Sheldon, was born in Chicago on September 25, 1932. For a famous writer, he is remarkably shy about meeting his public and has given few interviews. Little is known about his childhood except that in his teens he worked at Comiskey Park selling hot dogs and beer. He has stated that being a baseball player was a goal during his youth.[1] Silverstein's friend Jean Shepard has aptly speculated that he gained his sense of absurdity from such a close affiliation with the Chicago White Sox, the woebegone team with the intensely loyal following.[2] One can also imagine the wish fulfillment granted by his five weeks with the Sox during spring training in 1962, part of his assignment for *Playboy* during that time.

At some point in his adult life, Silverstein married, had a daughter, and divorced. During the Korean conflict in the early 1950s, he was stationed in Tokyo for military service as a contributor to and cartoonist for *Pacific Stars and Stripes,* a newspaper for personnel in the armed services. The year 1956 marks the emergence of Shel Silverstein as a professional cartoonist. His first contribution to *Playboy* magazine, entitled "sketches from the satirical pen of a talented new cartoonist," appeared in the August issue. The simple sketches, made with fragile lines and depicting faces only in profile, were more a collection of caricatures than a comic strip or an illustrated sexual joke, which he would later contribute.

Thereafter continued a long association between the cartoonist and *Playboy* that lasted until 1982, with contributions of cartoons and verse published sometimes regularly, at other times intermittently. Some of Silverstein's later books and poems were published first in *Playboy's* pages, then somewhat revised for the children's market. Silverstein's whereabouts from 1957 to 1961 are easily discerned from his cartoons for *Playboy,* in which he reported events from around the world: first from Tokyo, after returning to his station in the service; then from Africa in October 1959; and lastly from Alaska in 1961. The cartoons frequently show Silverstein himself committing various social gaffes as a result of his American assumptions, with occasional sexual asides. For example, while in London (October 1957) as *"Playboy's* wandering beard," he reported that Princess Margaret, then an unmarried young woman, was not interested in pursuing candidacy for Playmate of the Month, the feature nude centerfold. Some of the other jokes concern wearing different clothes, usually of questionable taste; being too frightened to enter a bullfight; and being pursued by a lion while on safari. As the series progressed and succeeded, the sexual innuendos became outright assertions.

Silverstein continued the pose of the foreign correspondent in some of his later contributions to *Playboy*. For example, he visited a nudist colony in 1963. His report, rendered in photos instead of sketches this time, showed the author and illustrator thoroughly undressed and at ease. He used the same guise of visiting correspondent to explore much less exotic locations, such as Greenwich Village, his home base at the time. His visits to Hawaii and Alaska took place when these two territories achieved statehood; trading on popular interest in these former territories and on wrongful assumptions about their primitive and frontierlike cultures, Silverstein investigated the natives' sexual habits as well as other cultural conditions.

This early cartooning was a disconnected apprenticeship for his later work for children, and though this early work has no *direct* bearing on the children's books, there are two obvious influences. First, the cartoons' captions all use a typeface that resembles that of a typewriter. This font, which mimicked a journalist's typing, also informed Silverstein's ideas about what the type in a Silverstein work should look like. The same typewriter font is found in nearly all his children's books, to greatest effect in the volumes of poetry, in which the font's wide, open look and the extra spacing between letters make the books easy to read and less text-dense in appearance.

The second influence is the cartoon medium itself. In his cartooning for *Playboy*, Silverstein experimented with framing an illustration and with the use of a limited space to convey his point. These experiences served him well in designing the poetry volumes. The lack of a frame around an illustration in a picture book suggests an experience that is easily entered into and that totally engages the reader. As Perry Nodelman has explained, cartooning emphasizes not beauty but rather emotion and action, which are the main concerns of Silverstein's poetry for children.[3] His illustrational style in the children's books is remarkably light, with little shading or crosshatching; the page's airy appearance, compared with the more ponderous, thoughtful styles of other illustrators and of some of Silverstein's own cartoons in *Playboy*, invites the viewer/reader into the experience and further engrosses him or her in the totality of the book. Silverstein's style has not developed much over his career, but his sure handling of the cartoon medium is clear both in the *Playboy* period and in his later works. Whereas other volumes of poetry are either unillustrated or heavily illustrated, with much color, Silverstein's choice of black-and-white illustrations is distinctive and originated in his work for *Playboy*.

After Silverstein's world tour, or perhaps during breaks between visits to various locales, three books from Playboy press reprinted several extended cartoons that Silverstein concocted from the stills of old movies, which he provided with his own captions. The Teevee Jeebie books reveal Silverstein as a television and movie addict determined to provide more humor to some familiar, maudlin, even boring cinematic situations. As Silverstein explains in his foreword to the first Teevee Jeebie volume,

> The next time you turn on your television set and find yourself confronted with an evening of vintage film fare so familiar you can almost recite the trite and true dialog before the actors do, try playing our new game, Teevee Jeebies. . . . Turn down the audio, and create your own scenario for the stirring scenes that move across your screen. . . . [T]he more active the imagination, the more fun.[4]

Thereafter follow two two-page spreads of various stills from identifiable and forgotten films with Silverstein's captions. Sometimes the humor is funny, but sometimes it falls flat on its face. Silverstein continued this captioning of old movies for several years, ending with "Who's Afraid of Teevee Jeebies" in October 1966. Most titles, such as "Bride of Teevee Jeebies" (1961) and "Gone with the Teevee Jeebies" (1962), are parodies of old movies. Silverstein usually used stills from the movie being parodied and then captioned them with an alternative script. *Playboy* first published these contributions in the magazine, then later collected and published them in three volumes. A series of one-liners, the books are not for reading through from cover to cover but simply for browsing and admiring the wit. The books were probably funnier in their own time than they are now; given the growth of both the television and the film media, the situations the cartoons depict would now be considered simpleminded and some of the humor juvenile.

Silverstein's early cartoons, primarily the wordless ones for *Playboy*, were collected and augmented in *Now Here's My Plan: A Book of Futilities*

in 1960. The book, which catalogs a number of aspiring and disappointed lives of varied inutility, also provides one of the few glimpses of
Silverstein the man, in the foreword by Jean Shepard. Oddly enough,
Shepard begins with the disclaimer "[Silverstein] is not for children, of
whatever age." Obviously this is the beginning of a joke: Shepard
implies that readers will have to determine their own adult status. Considering that Silverstein would soon embark on a career in children's literature, the disclaimer is shocking. Apparently, Silverstein's repertoire in
1960 did not suggest which of his talents would be realized in the
future; certainly the work contained in *Now Here's My Plan* does not
presage the output that is the concern of the present book.

However, Shepard is less wrongheaded elsewhere in the foreword and
gives a description of Silverstein as

> Neanderthalic: stocky, bearded, vaguely stooped, and unbelievably
> sloppy. Yet there is also a distinct air of imperious Edwardian dignity
> about him. He has a New Testament face that is strong and hawklike
> and that gives the impression that he is about to build an ark. Which is
> probably true. (*Futilities*, n.p.)

One has the sense that this is a personality larger than life, full of contradictions and ponderousness as well as of humor. His housekeeping is
nonexistent, his furnishing eclectic, and "[h]e lives in Greenwich Village
surrounded by things that go bump in the night," including, apparently,
things that may be living in his "digs," which are aptly named for the
piles of personal belongings in his home, as Shepard notes. One has the
overall impression of a creative, daunting talent raging to find expression on paper but restless and restive to the point of being unable to
focus long enough to work out the details. Shepard would place Silverstein in a league with writers Ring Lardner, Don Marquis, and George
Herriman if only his talent could be stilled long enough to find realization for others to enjoy (*Futilities*, n.p.). This foreword is one of the few
testimonials to Silverstein's personality; as Richard Lingeman says, "Mr.
Silverstein hates interviews, but he likes to talk."[5] Lingeman's article is
much less revelatory about Silverstein the man, but he does note the
poet's belief in fantasy only as fantasy, not as possibility, and in telling
children the truth about what they can expect in life.

In his three-part "History of Playboy," contributed to the magazine
in the first three months of 1964 on the occasion of its 10-year anniver-
sary, Silverstein gently poked fun at Hugh Hefner, the office staff, the

Playboy club, and the complexity of *Playboy*'s operation. At this point in his career, Silverstein also found other activities, including the children's books that are the subject of this volume, to occupy his interest. He also began writing songs and lyrics for such musicians as Johnny Cash and Loretta Lynn, recorded his own albums, and wrote original motion picture scores. These experiences show up in the easy rhyming and heavy rhythms of the poetry volumes; many of these poems lend themselves to memorization and performance in a way that makes children own the poems. One can imagine the poet trying out the poems aloud, as if they were lyrics first, then poems on a page. Silverstein's contributions to *Playboy* diminished as he pursued other interests.

Silverstein contributed occasionally to *Playboy* throughout the 1960s and 1970s, his last contribution, "The Twenty Commandments," appearing in December 1982. Given that this is the last of the *Playboy* contributions, it bears examination as a valedictory compendium of what makes the artist tick. The cartoon of Moses splitting the tablet in half suggests the possibility that he provided only the first 10 commandments. Here are Silverstein's other 10:

> Thou shalt not compromise
> Thou shalt not judge
> Thou shalt not seek rewards
> Thou shalt not follow leaders
> Remember every day to keep it holy
> Honor thy children
> Thou shalt not destroy thy body before its time
> Mind Thine Own Business
> Thou shalt not waste thy time
> Thou Shalt Not Lay Guilt Upon the Head of thy Neighbor.[6]

Considering that Silverstein's career is marked by cartoons and situations that suggest a lack of principles and high-mindedness, this is a remarkably sane and open-minded set of rules by which to live. It does not suggest wanton use of other people only for sexual purposes or exploitation, and it does suggest toleration and respect of people and privacy as a way to order human relations. The list consistently sums up the preciousness of life and living. This is no misanthrope, though that role is clearly part of Silverstein's repertoire; nor is this a depressing set of guidelines to avoid being hurt by life, though elsewhere Silverstein certainly teaches children to be wary of their fondest hopes and desires. It is clearly iconoclastic in its recommendation to follow no leaders and comments on the first 10 commandments as well as on Silverstein's own substantial accomplishment in writing for children, in the advice to respect children and to remember every day. Overall, it is the sane advice of a worldly wise man, who lives on, but not in print or interviews, in privacy this book will respect.

Because of the controversial subjects in Silverstein's writing for children, he has not received many prizes for children's literature. *Light in the Attic* received the Buckeye Award in 1983 from an association of educators and librarians in Ohio; *Sidewalk* received the Michigan Young Readers' Award in 1981 and the New York *Times* Outstanding Book Award in 1974. No Newberry or Caldecott Award, no honorary doctorate, no other traditional honor mark Silverstein's accomplishments. Perhaps the best indicator of what he has contributed to the field of children's literature comes from the New York *Times* best-seller list. Nancy Larrick, herself a poet for children, noted that as of April 27, 1986, *Light in the Attic* had been on the best-seller list for 164 weeks. As she comments, "It should be noted that rarely has a book of poetry made this prestigious list and never before a book of poetry for children."[7] Adding to the book's remarkable performance is its presence simultaneously on both the children's best-seller list and the adult list for a short time after its original publication. Few books for children, even with the built-in marketing that comes with an award, last this long, through several generations of children; no book of poetry has this draw, not even *A Child's Garden of Verses* by Robert Louis Stevenson, a classic of children's poetry that is showing its age. Silverstein the iconoclast has become more accepted in schools, libraries, and anthologies in recent years. Once part of an outcast coterie of fans and readers, the books are now recognized for their accomplishment and are even tolerated and sometimes taught in schools, one of the only places where poetry—as opposed to verse-poetry, the informal, "jump-rope" rhymes that children frequently sing—still finds currency.

More than 20 years have passed since the publication of *Sidewalk* and more than 15 since *Attic*, and yet both books of poetry are still best-sellers even though they are available in hardcover only. Not cheap paperback editions with inferior paper, these books with substantial price tags still occupy precious retail space and are still sold at full retail price in bookstores, not having been relegated to discount houses or remainder lists. Children's books rarely have such staying power; even rarer is the volume of poetry that stands the test of time. The rest of this book is a study of Silverstein's secrets for a long and prosperous life between the covers of his books.

Chapter Two
Trees and Lions and Prose

The books in this chapter herald Silverstein's initial entrance into the children's arena. *The Giving Tree* and *Lafcadio*, written in prose, are both allegories about human life. *The Giving Tree* remains popular for its sentiment about giving and for its appropriateness as a Christmas gift; *Lafcadio* is popular mainly with those adults and children who are intent on reading every Silverstein book available. In both books the author does not interpret the ending. If these are allegories about how to live life, they are not tightly didactic, nor are the lessons entirely clear. Perhaps the lack of clarity at the end is deliberate by the author, who has publicly eschewed easy, simpleminded answers and solutions; perhaps clarity was simply beyond him or was too difficult for a spirited iconoclast to control. In any case, these two books and three others of less accomplishment, which are dealt with at the end of the chapter along with the cartoons and books published in and by *Playboy,* formed the apprenticeship for the two volumes of poetry that established and maintain Silverstein's reputation among writers for children.

The Giving Tree

The Giving Tree was Silverstein's first book to be appropriated by children and their caretakers. Originally recommended on the dust-jacket flap "for all ages,"[1] the book has become a kind of cult favorite among college students, Christians, and gift givers. After the publication of the two volumes of poetry, *Tree* began to occupy space on shelves devoted to children's books in both libraries and bookstores, though it was not designed originally for a young audience. Perhaps the text's simplicity and the artwork's spareness suggest a younger audience.

Appearances can be deceiving. The book has such mythic resonances and yet such vague, undefined meaning that it is difficult to tell whether it is a cynical comment on charity and human relations or a commendatory fable on the satisfactions of generosity for the giver. Given the undercutting of the book's high-minded themes, two reviewers, Jacqueline Jackson and Carol Dell, claim that "it is hard to believe that anyone would take Shel Silverstein's The Giving Tree seriously, as an admirable story of selfless giving."[2] Although *Tree* is easily read as a parable of the satisfactions of giving, it may also be read as an antifeminist track about the submission of womanhood to male desire, as well as a sardonic judgment on the unbalanced nature of human relations and the obsessions of love. Like a fable, the story involves two characters, an apple tree and a boy. When the boy is young, he plays in the tree's branches, eats her apples, and sleeps in her shade. As he grows older, he spends less time with the tree and more with a young lady, whose toes are visible next to his in the tree's shade. Finally, in young adulthood, he leaves the tree. When he returns, he demands money, which she supplies by suggesting he sell her apples. For a time he is absent again, but then he returns and demands a house, so that he can marry. She gives him her branches so he can build the house. He returns again, much older and this time clearly disillusioned by life; he wants a boat to sail away from his troubles. Without anything else to give, the tree donates her trunk. When last he returns, he is too old to enjoy any of her earlier pleasures, which she admits she cannot give him anymore anyway. On the final page, the two find rest together when he sits on her stump.

Reader Expectations

The story originally found much favor among college readers, who saw it as a parable about perfect, selfless giving and its ultimate rewards. The high-mindedness of such a theme, the story's sadness and yet idealism, and the simple text had much appeal for a collegiate audience in the seventies that also found refuge in drugs and in the works of A. A. Milne. Once again, the dust-jacket flap copy interpolates in advance of reading that "this is a tender story, touched with sadness, aglow with consolation. Shel Silverstein has created a moving parable for readers of all ages that offers an affecting interpretation of the gift of giving and a serene acceptance of another's capacity to love in return." The reader is cued about what to expect in such a story—emotion and reciprocal affection. The cover features a bright lime green background, the tree and its leaves a darker tone of the same green. The boy's skin is white, but his short trousers and an apple falling from the tree are a rich red. The cover, which suggests a warm springtime, depicts the tree handing down an apple in generosity and the boy waiting with outstretched hands below to catch it.

The colors also suggest the green and red of Christmas, that period of consummate American generosity and commercialism. The choice to color the cover at all seems significant, especially in light of Silverstein's signature design of black and white for his other books. The book is one of only two Silverstein works with a colored cover, the other one more subtle, in beiges, and so stands out on the shelf among his other black-and-white books. The pictures between the covers, Silverstein's usual pen-and-ink drawings on a spacious white page, are reassuring in their recognizability as authentic Silverstein to a reader familiar with his other works. Perhaps the choice of colors is deliberately ambivalent, to evoke both spring and Christmas at the same time. The colors together, the scarlet of the apple and the lime green of the tree and its background, remind American readers of the joys of giving at Christmas; in fact, the book makes a good Christmas gift and is heavily marketed at that season for that purpose. Even the title controls the interpretation, as titles should, by focusing on the tree and her attributes rather than on the boy, whose requests might seem demanding and unfair if he were focused on in the same way the tree is. By evoking in advance the reader's focus and expectations about the story, Silverstein controls what the reader will perceive and how the reader will interpret.

The tree is the perfect giver, never expecting anything in return except the boy's visits. When he demands, she gives, even to the point of self-destruction. After giving her limbs in a selfless act that suggests self-mutilation, he is not satisfied but returns to request her trunk, which she also sacrifices in a suicidal gesture. Even though the story implies that the tree is lonely when the boy is not around, in the repetition of the single word "alone," she never reproaches him for his lack of attentiveness or even holds back her gifts of herself. She is a cheerful giver, one who has reportedly inspired many Sunday sermons.

Critical Response

The tree's attitude of self-abnegation has excited many critics. Of all Silverstein's books, this one has received the most critical attention. Much of this criticism has been negative, arising especially from women and minorities who see the tree's behavior as self-abnegating, even suicidal. Barbara Schram has called the book "dangerous" because it exemplifies the myth of the "happy slave" who does not see the exploitation of giving service without return. She worries about boys and girls seeing the tree's approval of selfishness in the boy and the tree's own female selflessness.[3] Even Jean Marie Heisberger and Pat McLaughlin, reviewers for *New Catholic World* and therefore, one may assume, proponents of Christian giving, point to the tree's masochism with disapproval. They warn readers that children would tend to identify with the boy rather than the tree; certainly the boy's pleasure in playing with the tree at the beginning is more appealing to the child reader than the passivity of the tree being played with.[4] Only an adult would be able to interpret the tree's action as central to the story's meaning, or certainly an older child who is knowledgeable about interpretative techniques and able to consider points of view other than the most obvious or most similar to his or her own.

It is possible that Silverstein is deliberately trying to make dual connections and second-level suggestions about the book's meaning, duping the reader by deliberately provoking a misreading. One sign that the author sends about such an intention is the back of the dust jacket, which features a black-and-white photograph of Silverstein wearing an ambiguous expression—is it pain? or a superior smirk? His appearance is not benign, as one usually expects of an author's publicity photograph on a dust jacket. Is Silverstein implying that the book is a joke, that giving, even in the spirit of Christmas, is not all it is reputed to be? Given Silverstein's sporadically misanthropic view of the human race in other books, this interpretation is entirely possible.

Silverstein deliberately twits the reader in one other place. The story ends with a picture of the old man sitting on the stump of the tree, back toward the viewer. The caption underneath this last picture is "The End," a clear marker for the reader that the boy, now the old man will make no more demands of the tree and that the tree is finally satisfied in giving. The old man is at the end of his life, though his satisfaction with life is hard to assess. But the picture shows "The End" in a more graphic way as well. The end of the tree is the stump, not exactly a glorious way to end life; perhaps the tree's life has been ended prematurely by her generosity to the man. The man's end is shown as well—his backside is clearly displayed, almost taunting the reader with a visual and verbal pun. Is the reader the butt of the joke? Or perhaps the old man is nothing but an ass at the end of life. Even with the clear announcement that the final page is "The End," the reader is tempted, by the book's rapid and rhythmic page turns, to turn yet another page, which is blank, and then to turn to the dust-jacket photo of the smirking author. Considering that the book ends with a joke, perhaps prematurely, and with an author in jest, how seriously should one take the story's implied message about the satisfactions of giving? The book ends asking more questions than it resolves.

Some critical commentary about the story concentrates on the way that the boy uses the tree for his own ends. He takes and gives nothing back, never returning the tree's love for him by doing something to help her thrive. Nature is an instrument with which he satisfies his selfish desires. Again, the boy is seen as an unethical manipulator, one who takes from life without concern and without giving in return until there is nothing left for him to take.

But the boy's desires do not seem frivolous, nor are his uses of the tree inappropriate. Apples are for eating; houses must be built, usually of wood; boats are useful as well as pleasurable; even a stump has its purpose. It is difficult to fault the boy's projects. And it is possible to find fault with the tree's attitude about being left alone so frequently by the boy. That is simply the way it is for trees, who have nothing else to do but grow and to do so outside the realm of human company. The story takes on its unsavory resonances only with the personification of the tree. As flora, the tree is treated with a healthy sense of nature's appropriate usefulness to humanity; as a human, she is abused and mistreated.

William Cole, a friend of Silverstein's who has anthologized Silverstein's poetry in several collections for children, and whom Silverstein thanked for his encouragement in *Where the Sidewalk Ends*, reviewed *The Giving Tree* shortly after it was published. Himself a poet for children, in the same sardonic, subversive, and slightly naughty mode as Silverstein, Cole is in a good position to judge the author's intent. As he says, "[T]he book, to me, is simply a backup of 'more blessed to give than to receive.' " As Cole admits, the general public's reception of the book has not indicated a popular assessment that the tree is stupid. However, Cole reports that his wife suggested "that the tree represents a mother, giving and giving with no expectation of return," an interpretation he rejects as feminine bias.[5] If even a colleague of Silverstein can publicly proclaim the story's ambiguity, perhaps that ambiguity is intended, though Silverstein has in various interviews, such as the one with Mercier, suggested that the book is just a simple story.[6]

Perhaps for a simple audience, one not paying attention to small detail, the story is as simple as the author claims. Certainly Silverstein has admitted a sentimental vein in his work that is unexpected from a writer so capable of castigating the human race in other works. But the book contains too many unanswered questions to be simply sentimental. The book is confounding from the start by the use of the pronoun *she* for the otherwise sex-neutral tree. Using *she* rather than *it* is a deliberate choice, especially since in the tradition of children's literature male characters are assumed to attract a larger audience because both sexes will identify with the adventures of a male. A female main character may eliminate half the readership. Without other reasons to choose females, authors generally default to using male characters.

The Nature of Love

Trees do not ordinarily suggest femaleness. At the beginning of the story, the omniscient narrator clearly states that the tree "loved" the boy, though the nature of the love is not as clear; is the tree the boy's playmate and lifelong friend? his obsessively devoted mother, whom he has learned to manipulate and to take advantage of? his childhood sweetheart and first love, who is left behind as the boy matures? The vague nature of their relationship is complicated by the fact that as soon as the boy begins to mature, he becomes unpleasant looking, with a demanding stance and a frowning face. Although the dust-jacket copy touts "serene acceptance of another's capacity to love in return," the reader does not see the boy returning the love. He never thanks the tree, never visits her in later life except when he wants something from her. Until the end of his life, when he is too old and too tired to want or do anything else, he does not stay with her or show any signs of concern or of being satisfied with what she gives him. At the end, he returns because he has nowhere else to go, not because he has any particular feelings of affection for her.

But perhaps William Cole's wife is right that the story is about a mother and her child. A mother's job is to eliminate her job, to let her children grow away from her. Part of this story's sadness is that the tree seems to have nothing else but the boy, and when he is absent, she is "alone," not necessarily lonely, though the narrative is open to that interpretation. The tree's pleasure in playing with the little boy is obvious from the outstretched limbs she extends to greet him when he first appears in the book. Her limbs reach out to protect him as he plays underneath her, they circle round him to catch him should he fall while climbing, and they hang down plaintively when he finally grows up and goes away. The gestures of the larger tree protecting and indulging the smaller boy clearly signal a motherly stance. This early section about their play is the only time in the book when the boy is declared truly to "love the tree," which is separated from the phrase "very much" by a turn of the page. The separation is an odd one—why the modifier at all? Does it intensify the love or diminish it? The page turn begs these questions, though the text provides no answers.

This is also the only time in the narrative when the declaration that "the tree was happy" is believable. The same statement appears every time the boy leaves with some new part of the tree in tow. Only at this early juncture is the tree's happiness unequivocal. But the picture accompanying this first declaration is of the boy carving a valentine into the tree's bark—"M.E. + T.," meaning "me and the tree." The image here is jarring. The boy declares his love by cutting into her, and she is satisfied with that tattoo of ownership. Carving initials into the bark of a tree will not do permanent damage, and the gesture is a traditional one of affection among the young. But using a knife on the skin of the beloved does not seem like a gesture of friendship, especially since the boy does not use it on himself, in some kind of childhood ritual of blood brotherhood. Rather, it seems like branding and thoughtless infliction of pain.

The nature of the boy's play may be an early foreshadowing device to indicate his basic nature. He collects the tree's leaves, in itself an innocent action, since he is shown catching them as they fall rather than plucking them from her. But he uses them to make a crown, something like the laurel wreath of a Roman emperor, so that he can "play king of the forest." Although this is a simple child's game of pretending power, the boy's choice of amusements indicates his desire to assume superiority and dominance over the forest, including the tree. The phrase "king of the forest" suggests the lion, king of the beasts, or the oak, king of the trees and therefore a superior being. The boy's nose is pictured arrogantly up in the air. Even in his early play, he indicates his need to dominate.

Besides permitting him to collect her leaves, the tree also lets the boy, sitting in the branches unseen to the outside observer, eat her apples, the cores of which he discards on the visible ground below. The boy does do the honor of taking off his shoes before he climbs her trunk, but this is the only sign that he takes into account the tree's feelings or dignity.

The boy's first demand of the tree, for money, sounds an acquisitive note. The boy wants the money "to buy things and have fun," marking the beginning of his indulgence in consumerism and of the tree's inability to provide for his needs directly. There are two two-page spreads that mark the passage of time before the boy makes his first demand: the first shows the boy growing taller, and the second shows the boy lying under the tree with another pair of legs—presumably female—and a new valentine carved on the trunk above the earlier one: "M.E. + Y.L."—young love? This picture also depicts the passage of time by showing two leaves falling from the tree, suggesting autumn, maturity, and perhaps the tree's resignation and anxiety about the boy's newly developing interests.

However, the tree/mother does not seem to recognize this passage of time and the boy's growing up. When he goes away the first time and returns, she greets him after an unspecified absence with the offer of the same activities they shared earlier—the boy's climbing on her, swinging, eating her apples. The picture of the grown man clearly shows that this is no longer a boy, though the tree addresses him as such. Here the boy makes his first request. This is also the first point in the book at which there are more than just a few words on the page. Here is the complication, the book's real narrative interest, and the tree and the boy converse at length about adult topics in an extended block of text. At this point Silverstein's story breaks away from the simple and uncomplicated. Without any small talk, the boy blurts out, "Can you give me some money?"

It is possible that the tree might have said no—after all, she has no means of getting money. Instead, she apologizes for her inability to supply his needs, as if trees normally possessed cash. She does give him the suggestion that he take her apples to sell, assuring both him and herself that if he has the money, he will be happy. Perhaps she is assuming the role of desperate mother, trying to please her child at almost any cost; perhaps she is a desperate lover seeking to please in order to regain his attention. In any case, she does not give him what he asks for, though she provides the means to get it. But in being resourceful in her answer, she denigrates her own abilities by pointing out that she has "only apples and leaves" to give him. Her willingness to give of herself is admirable here and difficult to fault, since trees normally and naturally provide fruit for those willing to harvest it. But she does apologize for things beyond her control. The first gift sets up a pattern of the boy demanding and getting in return and the tree's responsive pleasure in giving even though the boy seems only temporarily satisfied by the evanescent nature of the things he desires. This scene also sets up the pattern of the boy going away and leaving the tree without further thought until the next time he needs something, to which the tree responds with growing sadness.

The second time the boy returns, he is clearly a grown businessman, wearing a loosened tie and shoes (he has previously been barefoot) and now showing a receding hairline. This time, the man responds to the tree's offer of play with his own preoccupation: "I am too busy," he says, signaling his growing absorption in work and the outside world. But it is difficult to fault his desire for a house so that he can have a wife and children, normal expectations in the course of adulthood. What is unusual is the tree's offer of her branches for the house lumber, a gesture of extreme self-sacrifice, especially since the branches also function as the tree's arms; the request seems to result in amputation. However, the tree's tone in talking about the gift is clearly that of granting a favor: "you may cut off my branches." Even the way the tree responds to the man's request for a house sounds a new note of distance and formality: "I have no house," she says, rather than the more colloquial "I don't have a house."

Again, the tree enables the boy to get his wish, though she cannot give him a house outright. This time she does not apologize. It also is becoming clear that she will not get from the relationship what she wants, the companionship and togetherness of the earlier times, which is what her continued offer of playtime suggests. The house will also enable the boy to stay away permanently, which is clearly not her desire and is a likelihood that contrasts pitifully with the tree's shaking "with joy" when the boy returns. Cutting off the branches and helping the boy to move away have the same result: isolation, self-denial, perhaps even death.

When the boy comes back a third time, he is markedly older, with glasses, a fedora, and a briefcase, perhaps suggesting the baggage of his life. This time the tree is so pleased at his return that "she could hardly speak." Now the boy responds to the offer of play with the excuse of his age and sadness. Once again, he wants to get away, this time in a boat. He cuts down her trunk at the point between the two valentines, leaving his original one to the tree on the stump and carrying away the one to his girlfriend with the trunk to make it into a boat. Once again, the tree willingly sacrifices herself to the man in order to assist his escape, this time in an unequivocal gesture of self-sacrifice and death. All that is left behind is the stump with the old valentine, a reminder of their affection for each other earlier in their lives.

Reading the End

Because this is a fantasy story, the tree is not really dead, though there is not much life left in her. The boy returns again, this time at the end of his own life. The tree accurately points out that she has nothing left to give and can no longer offer even to play. But the man responds that he is too old to eat apples or swing in the branches or climb the trunk anyway. Such pleasures have no appeal for him anymore. The tree apologizes nonetheless, wishing "that I could give you something" and denigrating herself a last time: "I am just an old stump. I am sorry." But the now-withered old man who stoops wants only a place to rest—perhaps a tomb? This time, the assertion that "the tree was happy" with the old man sitting on her is difficult to accept if one takes into account all that she has given him and his final ignoble gesture of sitting on her as though she were a lowly piece of furniture. The tree's happiness at the end can be understood as unequivocal only if one assumes the unalloyed pleasures of selfless giving, that giving is its own reward.

At the story's end, both boy and tree are dependent on each other for happiness, or what little pleasure remains left to them in life given their mutual disabilities. The question is whether they are overly dependent. It certainly appears that the tree may be, since nothing seems to please her except the boy's return and the gifts she makes to him. But her gifts ensure that the boy will move away; although her gifts do not result in the boy's staying with her, as she might wish, she does nothing to make him feel guilty that he does not spend more time with her. She is also not trying to buy his attention, only gain his approval. On the other hand, her happiness clearly resides in his presence.

The boy is also an independent operator. He does not demand from her, only requests, though in tones that are unmannerly—no please, no thank you. The tree could refuse but instead makes counteroffers that result in her diminution. It is not clear whether the boy is happy with the end result of her gifts, but his absence after receiving her generosity suggests that he finds something more interesting to do than to stay with her. After all, he returns to the tree only three times over the course of his adult life. His requests of her also fit the kinds of activities humans find interesting at various points in their lives. But certainly neither the tree nor the boy finds permanent happiness until they are reunited at the end. Perhaps it is not the tree's ability to please the man at the end that ensures her happiness but rather his long-term presence.

The story's attractiveness for Christians is evident in the interpretation that sees the tree as a paschal offering. The tree certainly does not require anything in return for her gift of herself. In fact, she finds her happiness in the giving. There is no end to her generosity, even when she thinks there is nothing left for her to give. As an image of Christ, the tree performs well, even giving what she can suppose will result in her own death. It is difficult to say whether she saves the boy with her self-sacrifice, though at the end she provides rest and comfort to the man, who has otherwise found only short-term happiness. She is his final refuge.

The tree's willingness to give without expecting a return accurately describes what children sometimes seem to expect of parents and what parents may sometimes wish they could do for their children. Being the all-perfect giver, who takes satisfaction in providing pleasure to the receiver and who gives because he or she wants to, is what parenthood frequently demands. Unfortunately, the story also reflects the behavior of children whose demands are too frequently and fully satisfied—they are thankless and only expectant of more. But being a selfless giver is a lesson Americans frequently wish to teach their children; participation in charities is a notable American cultural trait that separates Americans from other, less charitable cultures. This book in some ways teaches children to give, to their own children, to those less fortunate, to those in need. Unfortunately, the book offers other competing lessons at the same time.

Perhaps the most devastating reading in the book results from a recognition of life's satisfactions across the span of a whole lifetime, for both the giver and the receiver. The man's life is unpleasant at least; he needs more all the time and at last looks only for a retreat, never having had enough satisfaction to say that he has had a good, full life. The tree is by herself, satisfied temporarily each time she gives but otherwise provided with no means for satisfying herself. At life's end, both man and tree are worn out, disabled, and anything but celebratory, even of the act of giving.

Finally, the careful reader is left with the conflict of the text with the visuals, the conflict of expectation of story with what is really there. That the book has so many different readings but that the simplest one prevails may be as much an indication of crisis in literacy, both visual and verbal, as a sign of the author's mixed intent. But Americans' penchant for a sweet, sentimental ending, especially in books for their children, has built *Tree*'s popular reputation, at the same time fueling the critical commentary. Peter, Paul, and Mary's rendition of "Puff the Magic Dragon" is contemporary with this book. Both celebrate the passing of the simple, breathtaking pleasures of childhood without mention of the less pleasant aspects of growing up and without any resolution about how one should look at maturity and adulthood. Both stories have been overinterpreted; Puff supposedly bears the burden of an allegory of drug use and abuse. In spite of the lack of resolution at the end of both tales, both continue to be popular for their supposed celebration of the best of life's stages and human emotions; yet close reading of both leaves a careful reader with ambiguous feelings. Those who are left behind as their little boys grow up—Puff and the tree—are objects of nostalgic sentiment.

Lafcadio, the Lion Who Shot Back

Lafcadio, the Lion Who Shot Back is the closest thing to a novel that Silverstein has written. Although the book's physical appearance indicates a substantial piece of writing, the length of the text is closer to that of a long short story or a novella. Certainly the book's packaging as a novel, with chapters and a substantial number of pages between a hard cover, aids the reader's experience of it as more than a vignette, though the book is not as long as a young-adult novel or an easy reader. A shorter version of the story, which originally appeared in *Playboy* in November 1963 (pp. 76–83), was contained on a short seven pages, which indicates the story's real heft, even of the apparently extended version between the covers of a book.

The story has a more intricate plot than the simple fable of *The Giving Tree* or even a longer poem in one of Silverstein's poetry collections. Lafcadio is a wild beast in the jungle, a sharpshooter who learns his skill on the gun of a hunter whom he has eaten. Whenever he needs more bullets to practice, he simply eats more hunters. Gradually, no more hunters bother the lions since their colleagues before them have mysteriously disappeared, and Lafcadio becomes the sharpest shooter in the world, by both his own estimation and that of a circus owner who finds him in the jungle and persuades him to return to the city.

Lafcadio enjoys his life as a celebrity and gradually becomes more like a man, with human haircuts and grooming, clothing, fancy foreign vacations, and an entourage of autograph seekers and female admirers. One day, he breaks down at the ennui of modern life and desires something new; his circus sponsor suggests hunting, and the lion finds himself confronted by another lion who knew him earlier. On one side are his fellow hunters, who urge him to shoot; on the other is the lion, who reminds him of his tail and his origins. Finally, Lafcadio walks away from the confrontation in confusion, never to be heard from again.

The story is clearly plotted, with Lafcadio becoming more urbane, cosmopolitan, and desperate for amusement as he becomes more human. But Silverstein's own voice intrudes on the narration in a characteristically digressive way. The book's full title, as it appears on the title page, is *Uncle Shelby's Story of Lafcadio, the Lion Who Shot Back*. Given Silverstein's autobiographical, hardly veiled presence in the story, the presence of the *Playboy* brand of humor, albeit slightly veiled, could almost be expected, especially by an adult reader. Although Silverstein appears to be telling a story to children in his Uncle Shelby persona, he does not resist the occasional humorous, slightly off-color joke for the older reader. For example, a reference to a before-bedtime drink of buttermilk and the subsequent behavior of the partakers as giddy and lightheaded surely suggest an alcoholic nightcap to a knowledgeable reader.[7] When the lion interrupts Uncle Shelby's night at home reading *National Geographic* and drinking hot chocolate, an adult familiar with the magazine's attraction for an adolescent fascinated with female nudity understands that Uncle Shelby is not reading the journal for its scholarly material alone. Finally, Lafcadio's pursuit by groupies suggests not simply women's star-struck behavior but their willingness to gratify their heroes sexually as well.

 ¯Uncle Shelby, the benevolent older storyteller, begins the book with a false start, restarts, recovers the same ground with the same false start, and finally begins the story. In the first person, he twits the reader with jokes throughout. The folksiness and specificity of the details give the story a sense of credibility and informal orality that is characteristic of Silverstein. Here the voice is less adult and teasing than in *Uncle Shelby's ABZ*, in which the wise, perhaps older child and certainly the adult reader will know that Silverstein is sardonically trying to con the child into suspending judgment and committing unthinkable, naughty acts that the child will regret. In *Lafcadio*, the voice is much more reliable and trustworthy. On one occasion, Silverstein claims that the child is actually present in the story at the time of the action though too busy watching a passing fire engine to notice Uncle Shelby walking down a busy Chicago street with a companion lion. The Uncle Shelby persona retreats into the story only rarely and only to reappear again shortly.

 Silverstein resorts to authorial intrusion—and in this case, invites the reader to intrude—to give a sense of veracity to his fantasy of a lion walking down some of Chicago's major thoroughfares. Such locations as Fifty-seventh Street and Dorchester Avenue and such dates as Friday, December 17 further cloak the storyteller's fantasy in the details of actual time and place. The adult reader may try to locate the specific places and times to see if there are any subtle jokes implied. As is the case with Silverstein's other writings, no particular benefit or meaning results from such a search; the Playboy Club is not on Dorchester Avenue, and Fifty-seventh Street has no world-renowned restaurants. The cuisine of the restaurant that the lion and Uncle Shelby visit also seems innocuous. The menu of stew, chops, and omelets reveals an eating establishment of no particular ethnicity or distinction. The restaurant is probably a generic one capable of producing conventional slow food, though the lion's preference for marshmallows all over everything makes it clear that the chef can be pressed to do more.

The story's overriding theme is the reverse of the feral-child syndrome: an animal never really becomes a human, and yet once he has contact with the delights and disappointments of human life, he cannot easily return to being an animal. In short, you can't go home. At the end of the story, Lafcadio simply wanders away from his dilemma of whether his loyalty belongs to humans or lions, never contacting Uncle Shelby again, though the narrator clearly expects a postcard. The open ending, in which the characters' final disposition remains unresolved, is a typical device of Silverstein's, especially when there is no humorous punch line available. Here, the ending avoids sadness by leaving open the possibility that Lafcadio may be happily preoccupied somewhere else, or that he has not been heard from because he has made his peace with being an animal. These are just speculations, though they clearly distract the reader from the lion's overwhelming sadness at being without kingdom, whether human nor animal.

That Lafcadio would consider being a hunter and going on safari with the expressed purpose of killing his own kind demonstrates the depravity that the pleasures of the human world can lead to. Lafcadio is so denatured by his contact with not only the human world but also the seductions of fame and wealth that he forgets that hunting his own kind is inimical. The opening of the book, in which Lafcadio as a young lion first confronts a hunter, demonstrates that the animals' antagonism toward humans is not innate; in fact, it is driven by humans' false assumptions that lions are natural man-eaters and that the only way to deal with them is to shoot them and make them into rugs. Likewise, the conflict between man and lion is driven by the lions' expectations, grounded in truth, that the hunters' only desire is to shoot them.

But Lafcadio is not like the other lions, who automatically run away from humans and their sticks that make funny noises. He questions leonine cultural assumptions and loves the sound of words; he is childlike in his naive assumption that hunters might in fact be interesting and perhaps friendly. With the charming ingenuousness of a child, he ponders the sound of the word *hunters:* "you know, the way some people like the sound of the words Tuscaloosa or tapioca or Carioca or gumbo, he liked the sound." In fact, Lafcadio develops a craving for marshmallows because of the way the word sounds; he has no previous experience of their taste. His wallowing in the sounds of human language, his perseverance, perhaps even obsession, with learning to be a sharpshooter, indicate his fancy for humans and their lives. His naiveté, combined with his nearly compulsive desire for the new and novel, leads him down the path to fame, money, human leisure, and dilemma.

But Lafcadio's examination and open-minded treatment of hunters does not reveal a new side to their personality. The picture of the first hunter he meets is one of Silverstein's ugly, slump-shouldered, mean-faced predators, who sees what he wants to in Lafcadio—a man-eater whose purpose in life is to be shot by the hunter. When he tells Lafcadio to put his hands up, the lion does so in a playful way, posing as if he were playing a game of statues. When the hunter's gun fails to go off because it is not loaded, he fully expects that Lafcadio will follow some kind of prearranged script, remain with his hands up, and simply submit to being shot. But with a child's petulance and an uncompromising clarity of vision, Lafcadio does not cooperate, pointing out that the hunter is "not nice," a distinct understatement, and eats him. The chapter ends with Lafcadio walking away from the viewer with the hunter's gun in his mouth. Although there is a sense of finality in the picture, of rounding off the chapter with both hunter and lion receiving their just deserts, the picture is also an example of one of Silverstein's naughty jokes: it shows the lion's bare behind, one of those visual jokes so frequent in the poetry collections. Clearly this is a lion, not a human, and therefore is not really naked, but the picture twits the viewer nonetheless.

In a child's enjoyment of the newness of all things, Lafcadio finds much pleasure in the small details of life among humans in the city. Like a child, he rides the hotel elevator up and down repeatedly, apparently also possessing the cast-iron digestive system of the young. He resists taking a bath, even though he "smells like an animal," just as he should. He resists (though eventually surrenders) because it is the childlike thing to do, though taking a bath is the first step in transforming himself into a human. After the bath he visits a barber and a tailor, who provide a manicure and a full dress suit respectively, to complete the transformation. He receives the services free of charge, the ultimate consumer indulgence, because of the power of his roaring; though he throws his power around, it seems inadvertent. In fact, he seems simply to be throwing a tantrum to get his way. The fact that he is a lion and therefore scares people into compliance is not known to him at this point.

After his stops at the barber and the tailor, Lafcadio experiences the ultimate civilizing experience for a lion or a young child: dinner at a fancy restaurant. Like an untutored child, Lafcadio blunders; since he is told that everything on the menu is quite tasty, he eats the menu; like a child whose palate responds to the familiar, he demands marshmallows—only marshmallows. In an attempt to provide a real restaurant experience, the waiter brings "southern-fried Marshmallow" and marshmallows boiled and scrambled, as well as "Marshmalloup (which is a marshmallow soup)" and several other versions of marshmallows, including "marshmeverything!" Silverstein is not above presenting dishes that are disgusting though interesting. In this case it is "a Marshmallow in tomato sauce" that provides the amusement through grossness that children produce in their own humor.

With a child's gusto for novelty and attention, Lafcadio enters the circus world. He becomes a world traveler, showing off his shooting ability and gratifying his fans. Gradually, he takes on the leisure pursuits of the rich and famous: scuba diving, golfing, "dancing in nightclubs with the most beautiful, beautiful girls," and vacationing on the French Riviera. His ultimate transformation comes with his ability to keep his tail curled up and hidden, except when he drinks buttermilk, that shorthand for alcoholic indulgence. He even does things that make him into a pun: he takes up writing and becomes a "literary lion." He becomes a "social lion," and his clothes are so carefully tailored that he becomes a "clothes lion." As Uncle Shelby concludes, "I suppose he was just about as happy and rich and famous as anyone could ever hope to be." The word "suppose" prepares the reader for what comes next: an unexpected, desperate call from Lafcadio to Uncle Shelby for something new and novel to do. It is not Uncle Shelby who suggests hunting and a safari as a cure for Lafcadio's ennui; rather it is Finchfinger, the circus man, who sells Lafcadio on the novelty and attractiveness of hunting. Lafcadio, who is crying and groveling when Uncle Shelby comes to his rescue, quickly grasps the idea with little thought to his origins. The word "hunting" is enough to remind the reader how Lafcadio got where he is now.

Lafcadio appears on safari completely humanized, fully clothed in safari jacket, boots, and pants; his hands are able to manipulate a gun, and he has no mane left. The only part of his lion nature that still remains is a whiskery mustache and goatee reminiscent of the lion's full beard. His tail shows slightly behind his safari jacket, just the evidence the other lion needs to verify that in fact this is a former lion acquaintance who needs some reality therapy. Once caught between human and lion, Lafcadio and Silverstein refuse to resolve where Lafcadio belongs, though it is clear that the delights of the human world have been fleeting, whereas the jungle, once the hunters are scared off by the sharp-shooting lion, is earlier described as Edenic, quiet, warm, leisurely, and without conflict.

But there is no criticism of Lafcadio's reveling in the pleasures of the human, civilized world. The problem is not that the lion enjoys human pleasures but rather that he becomes so human that he forgets his lion pleasures. Had Lafcadio simply gone to Africa to see the sights, the criticism of him would not be so ironically powerful. The conflict results from Lafcadio's naive acceptance of Finchfinger's enticement, when he first leaves the jungle, that Lafcadio can "make lots of money and . . . can be the greatest shooter in the world and . . . can be famous and eat wonderful foods and wear silk shirts and yellow shoes and smoke fifty-cent cigars and go to wonderful parties and have everyone pat you on your back or scratch you behind the ears or whatever people do to lions." When Lafcadio the naive counters with "What do I want with all that stuff?" Finchfinger rejoins, "Everyone wants that stuff." Although Silverstein's book does not question that everyone would want that stuff, he subtly points out that gratifying all one's desires does not make one happy or satisfied; in fact, it may just result in boredom and distortion of one's nature.

The complexity of the story's moral here is consistent with Silverstein's avowed purpose to not give children easy answers to complex problems or simpleminded endings that suggest that life's problems are easily solved. The attractions of the world are clearly celebrated here. Yet the "middle-aged" child will recognize the boredom and thirst for newness that Lafcadio suffers so devastatingly; even Mark Twain, in *The Adventures of Tom Sawyer* (1876), a book from a simpler age, notes the difficulty children have with keeping themselves amused. New things are always better, though the novelty wears off, and that which one does not have is infinitely more appealing than those things already in possession. In *Lafcadio,* even adults are included in those who suffer such needs for the new. The ending is not closed, but it is also not sad; thus it is appropriate for children, for whom tragedies are deemed too emotional.

The illustrations in *Lafcadio* are some of Silverstein's easiest and best; page layouts feature text in whatever place suits the illustration. The lion at the beginning looks more like a stuffed toy than a ferocious beast; his boneless elbows and forthright eye contact with the reader mark him as a guileless innocent who is willing to be open minded and friendly, whose body is lithe and flexible enough for him to become a sharpshooter as well as a rug. As he gradually transforms himself into a man, he looks more and more like Silverstein himself in the early *Playboy* cartoons he created while touring the world. The lion's casual slump of the shoulders, his development of dexterous hands in place of paws, his upright stance and hidden tail, his facial hair and receding hairline, all mark the urbane, worldly wise and blasé attitudes of the intentionally famous and rich, which emerge through the changes in the lion's physique. The loss of his head of hair, which dwindles to the goatee and brief mustache, signals to the viewer his thorough transformation. The illustrations take advantage of the two-page spread to show jungles and circus parades; the lion roars at adversaries from the left edge of the page, the compliant victim appearing at the edge of the right. The pen lines are in general light and sure, made with a caricaturist's deft hand, though in some of the landscape illustrations the pen lines become heavier and more dense and animals sometimes resemble primitive cave paintings in their bare, essential outlines.

Overall, the lion is a lovable, likable beast whose foibles are acceptable and whose happy end is devoutly wished for by readers both young and old. As a circus story, this one follows in the tradition of Toby Tyler, whose stories depict a young one who runs away and then realizes that circus life is not as great as he supposed. Unfortunately, Lafcadio is a lion, not a boy who can go home like the prodigal son when he finally reaches his realization. The transformation of lion to human is not easy, as it is with de Brunhoff's Babar the French elephant, who simply puts on a suit and imports French civilization to his jungle. Here Silverstein continues themes of the pleasures of pleasure seeking and humans' (and animals') need to keep moving on to new things in life. Above all, the quester needs to remember while in the process of the quest what it means to be natural.

The lion's pitiable appearance on the cover predisposes the reader and viewer to sympathy; though the picture is used in the text to show the lion's embarrassment at being told he is naked by the circus man, the lion's pose on the cover works equally well to hide him behind his knees and arms as he looks balefully at the reader. Overall, the book shows Silverstein's ability to address a child reader, to create complex situations in short order, and to provoke the reader into considering a complex dilemma. The sly voice of the tall-tale narrator presages Silverstein's strength in the volumes of poetry to come: creating and sustaining a varied and yet believable voice that is capable of humor and pathos between covers.

Lafcadio is an exact contemporary of Maurice Sendak's *Where the Wild Things Are;* 1963 seems to have been a popular time for stories about the effects of the wild on creatures and about how these creatures, animal in one case, human in the other, get back to their origins and reassimilate with their own kind. In Max's case in *Wild Things*, wildness is something he confronts and learns to accommodate and ameliorate. In Lafcadio's case, wildness is something he loses, to his unresolved and everlasting confusion. Being human is good in both books, but hanging on to one's wildness and learning to deal with it is a higher virtue in both books as well.

Other Rehearsals

The books discussed in this section show Silverstein's other efforts to address a child audience, with varying degrees of success. As a group, they are further evidence of an apprenticeship in various formats for the success to come in the poetry volumes. In *Who Wants a Cheap Rhinoceros?*, Silverstein's development over the course of his career as a children's writer is most evident. The book was first published in 1964, before the success of the poetry volumes, then revised in 1983, after their publication. In its revised and expanded form, the book shows Silverstein developing a softer, more sentiment-filled approach to his work for children. The book is about the suitability of a rhino for a pet. The rhino fits the requirements for a pet immediately not only because of its availability at the right price but also because it is the ultimate playmate, more than a pet. In a series of two-page spreads, the rhinoceros shows that it is a comfortable sleeping companion and a healer of hurts both mental and physical. It is also willing to run interference against parents, who might complain about grades should the rhino not eat the report card first and who might punish, except that they will not be able to overcome the rhino's fierceness in protecting his boy/owner/playmate. The rhino is also unpredictable in that it eats the table along with the table scraps and hides in the strangest places, like the toilet, during hide-and-seek. It also acts as a plaything, willing to be dressed up as a girl for Halloween, albeit not completely accepting the sex change. Part of the fun of this playmate is its unpredictability; its leading physical trait, the proboscis, can be a coat hook, or it can be a disguised footprint: in the latter case, instead of leaving rhino tracks all over the house, the rhino puts a shoe over the proboscis and turns upside down, hopping like a pogo stick and leaving a misleading human shoe print instead. This is one of the book's slyest moments: the rhino claims to be particularly tidy in its movements about the house but instead implicates someone else by its mischief, leaving a trail of human prints instead of rhino prints.

And yet as slyness goes, this is not a particularly crafty, naughty act. That is the key to this book, because this rhino's most important qualification as a pet is that "he is easy to love,"[8] as the last page tells the reader, who has already been largely persuaded of the rhino's appeal. Though the themes of hugs and love appear in the poetry volumes, they do not receive as much weight as they do here because this book ends in the embrace between a boy and his pet, the proboscis lending itself to a loving stroke from the boy. The book has many of the same themes as the poetry volumes: tricking adults, especially parents, and playing tricks, though the toilet joke is about as off color as the humor gets. But the ending embrace and the repeat of this picture on the dust-jacket cover—the hug at the end of the book is also its introduction—makes the book a gentler, more consistently and mildly humorous work than the earlier poetry volumes or the earlier edition of the *Rhino* book itself.

The colors of the dust jacket, two tones of tasteful beige along with a deep rose accent, mark this book as different from most other Silverstein works for children, which are starkly black and white. This book is tasteful, gentle, and clearly geared for a young audience of early readers, whose parents are likely to censor and purchase their books for them. The rosiness of the accent color on the cover accentuates the warm, fuzzy feelings inside, in spite of the rhino's more violent reputation. There are only two places in which the rhino's ferocious reputation manifests itself: in one, he steps on the boy's foot accidentally; the accompanying picture, of a boy holding his foot and crying in pain, is repeated on the back of the dust jacket, a mild criticism, at the child's expense, of the rhino's suitability. The other incident occurs when the rhino threatens, but does not actually menace, the boy's mother when she goes to discipline him. The tension throughout, between what the rhino might do and what he actually does, carries the book's interest. And the cheapness alluded to in the title never becomes an issue.

The book's typeface, a large, rounded roman face with wider letter spacing, slightly more decorative, angled serifs, and in a larger point size than the one in the poetry books, is an amalgamation of a typewriter font, a schoolbook font, and something more elegant. This book is the most elegant, least objectionable of all of Silverstein's works for children.

A Giraffe and a Half shows what *Rhinoceros* might have been: a large, less expensive picture book with less attention to the bookmaking.[9] *Giraffe* is another story about a pet, but the story is told in consistent cumulative verse that adds detail after detail to the story. It is quite a long book, is printed on cheaper paper than is *Rhino* in its current edition, and is exclusively black and white with no accent colors. The typeface is atypical for a Silverstein book: a bold, blocky helvetica face with no serifs, no elegance; it is simply a plain, blaring face with no particular artistry. One might have expected such a face, which is bold, in the book's headings or titles, but it is used throughout, to drab effect. The book looks cheap, though there is nothing in the story that demands such a transitory, newspaperlike design.

Nevertheless, the story is an interesting one: the young giraffe of the title is the pet of a little boy; when the two get in a tussle over which way to go, the tether around the giraffe's neck becomes a line for tug-of-war, and both parties' exertion on the line is so great that the giraffe stretches by half to become the title of the story. He simply matures by growing his neck. As he and the boy proceed through the story, they confront a parade of events trailing from left to right: a skunk, a wagon, and a whale all add to the growing confusion and riotousness on the page. Suddenly, at what would seem to be the end of the story, all disappear down a hole. Yet all the characters and their appurtenances reappear from the hole, and the giraffe sheds them, one by one, even shrinking away his half, until at the close of the story he is just a giraffe. The boy, who has been a dubious participant in the precarious hilarity of the addition and subtraction of hangers-on, is clearly pleased by the story's ending—his pet is just a pet again, and a young one at that. On the book's last page, both he and the giraffe gaze approvingly out at the reader.

The success of this story is much like that of Dr. Seuss's *And To Think That I Saw It on Mulberry Street* (1937). In short lines with internal rhyme, the imagination of *Giraffe*'s narrator accumulates things in breathless progression. But *Giraffe* goes Dr. Seuss one further: at what seems to be the precipitous and definite end, the story begins again, although the second half proceeds much more expeditiously to its end; *Giraffe* ends where it starts, with a feeling that it is indeed well plotted. These two pet books together show Silverstein's experimentation with an audience younger than that intended for his volumes of poetry. Although these are fine storybooks, they are not outstanding ones; a single, linear story and a large two-page spread do not give Silverstein enough opportunity for complexity or for experimenting with different formats, layouts, and voices. Further, the level of humor is much simpler than that which school children, as opposed to the preschoolers for whom the picture books were written, will find most attractive. Silverstein's strength in the volumes of poetry lies not in the extended poems but rather in the short ones. And yet both these picture books show Silverstein's strength in telling a story that proceeds expeditiously, and both books succeed where *Tree* and *Lafcadio* fail: at their endings. These books have endings that tie the story up with a big red ribbon, tidily and effectively. No great meaning is hidden or obvious; the story is good fun and the ending satisfies. *Giraffe* succeeds as technically proficient verse: the rhymes are neat, not forced or inexact. *Rhino*, on the other hand, starts as verse and then moves into prose.

Both books, because of the success of the poetry volumes, remain in print 30 years after their initial publication. On the other hand, *Uncle Shelby's Zoo: Don't Bump the Glump!*,[10] another animal-story picture-book experiment, is the only one of Silverstein's early picture books not to be reissued. Perhaps the public's willingness to keep purchasing such books by Silverstein was simply overextended by the time it was published. *Rhino* and *Giraffe* prepare today's beginning readers for the pleasures of the volumes of poetry they will be able to read for themselves when they are a bit older. At the time of their initial publication, they were experiments by an emerging voice and pen and pale harbingers of the success to come in *Sidewalk* and *Attic*.

Uncle Shelby's ABZ: A Primer for Tender Young Minds is the transition piece between Silverstein's work in *Playboy* and his work for an audience of children. Most readers will find it fairly distasteful, since the humor is satiric and the butt of the satire is usually children. The *Z* in the title is deliberate: this is an offbeat, discordant alphabet book designed more for knowing adults and sophisticated older children than for the younger preschool readers who are the usual target audience for an alphabet book. For example, *G* is for gigolo,[11] not a word that most adults would introduce to children. In the book, Silverstein urges children to eat lots of green apples and to drink black ink. The avuncular narrator's voice never pretends to sound authentic or credible to children but rather is sarcastic and sometimes sinister, like an unpleasant, older bully and con artist. There is no warm, sympathetic feeling toward children, especially very young ones, in this book. This is a "funny" uncle who teases children to do things that they would be unlikely to do on their own but that the elder adult voice recommends, to their detriment. The view of human relations here is not that of Silverstein's "Twenty Commandments" but rather closer to the one found in *Now Here's My Plan* and the *Playboy* cartoons in which that book has its origin: others are to be distrusted first and trusted only intermittently. There is little hope of real permanence or joy in the world. This adult seeks not to befriend but rather to trick and tease with superior verbal skills and world knowledge and bad logic. Getting the best of someone, getting another into trouble and luring others into trouble in the process, all the while maintaining one's distance from blame, are Uncle Shelby's primary modi operandi.

The book is hand illustrated, hand lettered, and not particularly orderly or neat in page design, giving it the appearance of a series of nasty, threatening notes rather than of the formal, spacious, thoughtfully designed pages that Silverstein shows himself capable of elsewhere. In some ways, the enjoyment of the book resides in the same reader processes that operate in A. A. Milne's Winnie the Pooh and Christopher Robin series (1924–1928). John W. Griffith and Charles H. Frey identify in those books "concentric circles of knowingness,"[12] in which the book's characters have limited knowledge, but the reader's greater maturity makes the humor visible and possible. In *Uncle Shelby's ABZ Book,* Silverstein patronizes an apparently young reader, who is naive enough to be tricked by the narrator's seductive but malign voice; a more mature reader, even an older child, the intended reader, can see the book's dynamic and enjoy the humor at the younger child's expense.

In some ways, the book is a rehearsal for the kind of humor evident in the poetry volumes. The victimization of younger siblings in the poetry comes close to the victimization here. Uncle Shelby and the older child know better than the little kid who might innocently approach an alphabet book as a beginning reader might. Silverstein's great strength in his poetry is in the collusion between the older child reader and himself, in understanding and knowledge that is superior to and more authentic than that of almost everybody, adults included. In these concentric circles, Uncle Shelby and the older child are clearly the most superior beings in all the world. In this older child, Silverstein finds his ideal audience for both his humor and his more serious statements.

Chapter Three

What Goes on
Where the Sidewalk Ends

Having shepherded Shel Silverstein through *The Giving Tree* and having teased out of him two picture books for children, Ursula Nordstrom, famous editor of children's books at Harper and Row, began to work with Silverstein on *Where the Sidewalk Ends*. The love-hate relationship between editor and free-spirited poet is recorded from both sides. From Silverstein comes the dedication of the book "To Ursula," the words in a helium balloon that a sharp-beaked bird threatens to swoop down on and pop.[1] In Nordstrom's own words about her career as a children's-book editor, "The finest authors have their young selves emotionally and easily available to them, and that doesn't always make for an emotionally mature and reasonable person."[2] *Sidewalk* itself shows no visible signs of whatever difficulties may have occurred during its editorial stages. Of the more than 100 poems in this volume, 19 are listed as having been published elsewhere; others, such as "The Worst," are totally rewritten from earlier versions in *Playboy*.[3] This volume is truly an anthology of poems from several years, not intended for publication in this collection but rather inspired by other events. The breadth of subjects covered is remarkable and marks the beginnings of Shel Silverstein the poet of childhood. Having elsewhere appeared as the snide Uncle Shelby or the high-living cartoonist for *Playboy*, Silverstein emerges here as a new voice of variety and veracity about modern childhood, unencumbered by expectations of what poetry for children should be, determined to tell what a child's life is.

Book Design: Beginnings and Endings

This book, despite its apparent lack of organization—there is no table of contents, no obvious authorial arrangement of poems—is shaped and organized for readers quite deliberately and to good effect. It has a beginning, the poem called "Invitation" (9), a cover picture that is repeated from a poem in the middle of the book, a title poem, which is not the one that accompanies the picture on the cover, and three poems at the end that constitute the book's closure. The other organizing principle is the two-page spread, which sometimes features just one poem with a large illustration, sometimes several poems grouped thematically, with interlocking, complementary illustrations. Although the book at first glance appears random, it is not; surely the editor had a hand in arranging its poems, though Silverstein's ability to illustrate across a two-page spread is certainly evident.

The opening poem, "Invitation," signals to an adult reader that this is a conventional poetry collection, at least as far as its arrangement is concerned, with a beginning and probably an ending. For the child reader, the poem not only introduces the convention of the introductory poem in a volume of poetry but also establishes the poet's voice as one that is comfortable with children, accessible to them, inviting without being patronizing. One of the keys to the book's success is this voice, which is pliable and varied but always accessible for the child reader. "Invitation" suggests that the book is like a building, with the first poem as a kind of doorway through which the voice of the poet beckons. The door is open for particular kinds of people, most especially dreamers but also storytellers from a wide variety of storytelling traditions. The tone of the poem is wistful and enchanting, creating the feeling that poetry casts a spell, which is in fact the case.

But there are some word choices in this poem that jolt the reader who is expecting a simple, spellbinding experience. The most unusual word is "liar": "If you are . . . a liar, / . . . come sit by my fire." The word differs sharply in its connotations from the more altruistic evocations of the words "dreamer" and "wisher." But liars, tall-tale tellers, are part of a long and honored American tradition of telling stories that are more outrageous than any others. Storytellers are honored as being the best when the stories they tell are the best—or worst—lies. The liar in this poem keeps company with the "pray-er," another odd coupling, since those who are seriously religious do not usually have much in common with liars. "Pray-er" must also be hyphenated in order for its meaning to emerge: the word is not "prayer," the speech made to a higher power, but "pray-er," the person who makes the speech.

But dreamers, liars, pray-ers, pretenders, and even the "magic bean buyer," who recalls the dupe Jack and his beanstalk story, all have something in common: their ability to communicate to others a situation, to create a tale in an outstanding way that is meaningful to the listener—

even to God—and to express a desire for an alternative version of reality that is convincing, at least as long as their stories are being told. These kinds of storytellers conceive of a world that is better than the everyday, and like poets they present that world for others to enjoy. Some, like the pray-ers, are more ardent and sincere than the liars and pretenders. But in all cases, these storytellers' skills are not just in imagining the world but also in making it accessible and enjoyable to others.

The image of the magic bean buyer is the first in Silverstein's consistent pattern of borrowing images from other literature for children, both poetry and prose. Here, Jack's act of being conned is celebrated, as it is in the beanstalk story, for the simpleminded prescience it signals; at some level, Jack trusts the people that he should and puts himself in the way of his own good luck. The beans are, after all, not simply beans, and his belief in their power leads him to good luck, courage, and fortune. By following the path of the naive simpleton, one can find magic, adventure, riches, and a good time in an evocative story.

The poem's borrowed imagery continues with an invitation to the reader not only to enter the door but also to sit at the fireside and join in the telling of "some flax-golden tales." Spinning gold out of flax is what Rumpelstiltskin does for his damsel in distress. Silverstein uses this borrowing more to conjure the image of spinning a yarn, as in spinning a good tale, than to evoke a reminiscence. Since the time when women spun thread at the fireside while telling stories, spinning has been associated with compelling stories. The "flax-golden" image lends the feeling of preciousness, excellence, and antiquity to the kinds of stories that result from such spinning. The invitation to join the various kinds of storytellers around the fire is encouragement for child readers to be storytellers themselves as well as to join in the experience of the others' tales. The repetition of the line "Come in!" indicates the eagerness with which newcomers will be welcomed into the experience of the book. Overall, the invitation to the book is a powerful one that draws the reader into an experience that is gratifying, ghostly, and honoring of the child's own ability to amuse by telling stories and making poetry.

What the poem does not suggest is the raucous, humorous tales contained in the volume. But in encouraging the reader's own storytelling ability, Silverstein begins what will be a consistent message in the book—that the child has the ability to create, imagine, and communicate his or her own interesting stories. The poem serves to open the door and get the reader into the book, no small task, as children do not always have open minds about what poetry may be.

The accompanying illustration of a tall candle burning in an antique candlestick, used in the days before electricity for both reading and lighting the way to the bedroom, calls forth the antiquity of the story-teller's role and signals the nighttime quality of long storytelling sessions. The candle is obviously burned down somewhat, indicating a story session already in progress but also symbolizing the light that a story gives to human existence and the light that a storyteller bodies forth. The candlestick illustration is repeated at the end of the book, after the index of poems on an acknowledgment page, which in other volumes might appear at the beginning: Silverstein acknowledges debts and gives thanks for encouragement, first to another children's poet, William Cole, who has elsewhere anthologized Silverstein's poems, and again to Ursula Nordstrom. Perhaps the candle burns as a tribute to their human accomplishments, too, or perhaps the illustration is repeated as a way of bringing the book full circle, rounding it off; the two candlesticks stand like open and close parentheses to the book's contents. In any case, the illustration is simple yet highly evocative and is used to good effect in the book's overall design.

As mentioned previously, there are three closing poems, spanning three two-page spreads, which slow the rhythm of the book and end the volume with an open conclusion. All three are short poems. The first, "My Beard" (163), is a limerick about a naked man with a long beard that covers his "bare" as he cheerfully saunters from left to right across the straight-line horizon at the bottom of the page. Nakedness is a source of much humor for children in grade school. The figure, whose posterior is slightly visible, moves easily from left to right, swiftly and without concern, focusing on the distance to the right and paying no attention to the viewer. His nudity echoes two themes Silverstein carries out through the volume: first, that naturalness is a virtue, and second, that nudity is a fit subject for children's poetry, though it is slightly scandalous and always humorous. The incorrect grammar, so lightly used and almost unnoticeable in the poem's rapid pace—"I never wears no clothes," which rhymes with "I goes"—is characteristic of the volume's informality and casualness about nudity. The naked little man lopes across the page into open space, to the end of the volume. His figure is repeated on a blank page following the index at the end, again a visual twitting of propriety and of the usual formal send-off and conclusion to a volume of more serious and conventional children's poetry. The man's end is the end. Indeed, he is such a fitting ending for the volume that the reader is surprised to turn the page and find yet another poem. "Merry . . ."(164) is a poem of perspective that contemplates the fate of a Christmas tree after Christmas is over. The theme here is hardly original in children's literature. Hans Christian Andersen's "Little Fir Tree" investigates the vanity of a potential Christmas tree, which is beautiful in nature but whose only aspiration is to be decorated for the big event; after the holiday, the tree, in desperate, sentimental isolation, is cast aside with nothing now to decorate him and no future, abandoned as refuse in an alleyway. In Silverstein's poem, the situation is less overwrought. Although the picture shows a withered tree, with dropped needles, prostrate limbs, and damaged star, the poem is not long enough to sustain the kind of teary excess in Andersen's ending. The ellipsis points following the title suggest the poem's downward path of emotion, akin to the mood of the aftermath of the Christmas holiday. Two central lines in the poem point to Silverstein's message: "No one's talkin' brotherhood, / No one's givin' gifts." Whereas the message of continuing the Christmas spirit throughout the year might be cloying in another context, here it is dealt with quickly and summarily so that the excessive sentiment found in Andersen is not possible. Yet at the same time, Silverstein repeats other themes in the word "brotherhood": dovelike conscientious objection and acceptance of racial and ethnic difference. This is a poem that might have been the ending to the book, though an untraditional one since it begins after Christmas is over but when there is some story yet to tell.

The book's final poem is not exactly an antidote to the sad, wistful, contemplative ending of the poem about the Christmas tree in March. "The Search" (168) suggests in its title Silverstein's aversion to tying up a book or a life with any kind of finality. The process of life is what is interesting, not the product or the final attainment of some desired end. For Silverstein, pat endings are always ultimately unsatisfying and transitory and are simply the beginning of yet another quest. The search under consideration here is the quest for the rainbow's pot of gold. The speaker, after a long quest described in two lines that repeat the word "searched" six times, finds the treasure but only fleeting satisfaction in having attained his goal. The poem's final line, "What do I search for now?," is a question left for the reader to answer and at the same time accurately describes Silverstein's attitude toward life and childhood. Stasis is undesirable. Goals, no matter how ardently wished for, are fleeting once attained. Movement, even without direction, is always better. Life is for moving through, though there are temporary points of reflection and fulfillment along the way. The pot of gold in the illustration accompanying the poem is positioned at the bottom of the left-hand side of a left page, facing a blank right one. Perhaps Silverstein is suggesting that the reader is now empowered to fill the right page with whatever he or she may find satisfying to search for next.

Finality and closed endings are typical in children's literature, even in children's volumes of poetry, many of which include a classical envoi poem to send off the book to its readers. But Silverstein is deliberately evasive here about ending the book; he deliberately violates expectations and conventionality. If there is an overarching theme to Silverstein's work for children, it is this violation of expectation. That he is deliberately flaunting convention seems obvious in his acknowledgments page at the end of the volume and in his photograph on the back cover: he looks out at the reader with his foot foremost, almost threatening a kick, a glowering grimace on his face. Again violating convention, the illustration on the front cover begins on the back, at the edge of the author's photo, and continues around, as if the book's experience is too large to be confined to a set beginning and end. The final open-ended question at the end of the book repeats the author's aversion to finality, as seen in his two earlier books. But the ending question also reiterates the theme of children's abilities to create for themselves and to shape their own lives in interesting if unusual patterns.

Overall, the opening and closing poems frame for the reader a collection that is particularly encouraging of reading and imagining. Only the poem about the man with the beard is typical of Silverstein's *Playboy* career. Instead, these poems are reflective about human nature and human motivation in telling stories and seeking out stories worth telling. Only the bare-man poem is tight in its rhyme and meter; in the other poems, Silverstein resorts to the easy method of creating rhyme by simply repeating words. In sum, the effect of the verse in these poems is easy, perhaps suggesting at the book's critical junctures the reader's own ability to create a satisfactory imitation; if poetry is this easy, one can write poetry this good by oneself, with little prerequisite skill or practice in complex rhyme or meter and with simple, easily understood subject matter, grammar, and diction. Of course, Silverstein's lack of technical precision and excellence has called down criticism from children's-book professionals. Silverstein's own answer would probably be that he doesn't really care what the pros think.

Title Poem, Cover Illustration

The opening and closing poems are not the only framing devices in the volume. The book's cover illustration, which really begins on the back, shows a city in the distance, with the foreground wrapping around to the front cover to the real subject of the picture, two children and a dog on the edge of a cliff. The sign, which the children and dog have ignored, says EDGE/KEEP OFF! and suggests that this volume is about poetry on the edge or over it. The poetry inside develops themes that are sometimes common to children's poetry—the cautionary tale; the poem of advice; poetry about school and common events and experiences in children's lives, such as holidays and conflicts with siblings and authority figures; and common effects, such as shadows. All of these themes are in keeping with traditional poetry for children in the English language, which is highly didactic or sometimes cloyingly sweet, as in Robert Louis Stevenson's *A Child's Garden of Verses* (1885). But Silverstein pushes the edges of propriety, sometimes deliberately violating etiquette and custom, going to the edge of what is acceptable in children's behavior and of appropriate topics for children. The cover picture, especially because it features the deliberate though humorous imperiling of the children and dog, signals that this is a volume not in keeping with other more sedate collections of poetry for children.

Inside the book, this illustration does not accompany the poem "Where the Sidewalk Ends," as the cover might imply. Instead, it is the two-page illustration for the poem "The Edge of the World" (88–89). Here the illustration is slightly altered: there is no boy at the edge of the precipice, looking over the edge in wide-eyed horror. Instead, a girl investigates the edge and looks beyond it, not under it as the boy does, to the perils of open space beyond her. Silverstein also adds some flowers, an earthworm, and a hydrant, all of which protrude to the underside of the cliff and heighten the peril and fantasy. A bird squawks out his anxiety over the situation.

The poem deliberately twits schoolchildren's learning erroneously that Columbus discovered that the world is round. Here, the narrator issues an incorrect correction, though it is not entirely clear whether the speaker is an adult or the girl in the illustration on the edge of the ledge and the edge of the world. Perhaps Silverstein deliberately does not make a distinction. In either case, the appeal to the reader is based on common sense and on the illustration's emotional content. The girl can clearly see that there is an edge to the world and that the world has a definite stopping place. The world's flatness is clear from the picture's straight horizon, which extends across nearly the whole of the two-page spread. The poem's narrator appeals to his or her own experiences in world travel, for he or she has "[s]at on the edge where the wild wind whirled, / Peeked over the ledge where the blue smoke curls" (89). Because he or she has gone to the edge, the assertion at the end that "The world is FLAT!" is credible. The message contradicts what children are taught in school. Even though the narrator condescends to address the reader as "boys and girls," using a particularly superior tone, the assertion does bear out what children experience every day—a more or less flat world, not a globe.

The poem, a simple one, makes an easily perceived joke at authority figures' expense that almost any schoolchild will appreciate. There is no attempt to be particularly poetic, with the possible exception of the alliteration in the line "the wild wind whirled," which rhymes with the ending word "world" in the previous line. The description of the whirl-wind and the smoke at the end of the world is consistent with the common collocation "to the ends of the world," which is where medieval map makers thought that the winds originated. The confidence with which the narrator describes adventures and the wildly romantic image of the edge of the world suggest that such a journey is worth the effort. But the commonsense assertion at the end debunks authority, though humorously. Silverstein's purpose here is simply a joke, not a rewriting of history and geography. Children can laugh at such a poem and still understand the truth of what Columbus believed. American children's experience as citizens of the New World that Columbus and others dis-covered for Europeans confirms his position as an authoritative figure in history. Although the cover illustration does not accompany the poem for which the volume is named, the repetition of the illustration creates a certain predictability. What is on the cover is what is inside the book, and the themes of subversion of authority, laughing at adults, and push-ing acceptability and control to the edge are introduced.

The title poem, which actually appears earlier in the volume, is unac-companied by illustration and faces another page without illustration;

the text-dense appearance of pages 64 and 65 indicate that Silverstein is just beginning to develop his ability to design a book that is both visually and poetically appealing to children. This unillustrated two-page spread shows his lack of full control over the dual media in which he operates. It is also possible that "Where the Sidewalk Ends" is a poem better left unillustrated, since readers' invented illustrations would likely be much more satisfying than an idiosyncratic interpretation of Silverstein's words that might limit the imagination. The poem describes "a place where the sidewalk ends / And before the street begins," which in some American dialects is called a "park" or a "walk" or sometimes even a "median," though the latter is a term more often used for a strip of green between two traffic lanes. In many American dialects, the strip between the sidewalk and the street has no name at all. Silverstein's decision not to name this area leaves much potential for fantasy. Without a name that fixes the strip in the imagination, it can be made into anything that Silverstein wants it to be. The grass here is not a normal shade of green but "soft and white," and it is the touchdown for a "moon-bird" who stops to feel the "peppermint wind" blow. Having developed the characteristics of the slender space in the first stanza, Silverstein continues in the second by developing the scenery on the other side of the sidewalk: it is urban, dirty, and full of places where "asphalt flowers" characterize the vegetation. The narrator takes the reader away from this urban blight of darkness on a stately walk that follows "chalk-white arrows"—perhaps suggesting children's chalk drawings on concrete—to the edge of the sidewalk.

The closing stanza ends with an inconclusive yet highly suggestive couplet: "For the children, they mark, and the children, they know / The place where the sidewalk ends." The assurance here that children do in fact know that there is something special and magical in that place, that they have some prescience about a space that for most has no name, invests in children a Wordsworthian superiority in their youthful but knowledgeable state. Children are vested with the understanding that the space is an antidote to the urban blight on the other side. Silverstein suggests that children have the right point of view about reality, which is unpleasant at best and should be avoided by going to magical, imaginative places. The solemnity of this poem, in contrast to many of the book's more humorous, more specific poems, gives both the book's title and the poem seriousness and dignity, especially relating to children's innate abilities.

"Sidewalk" is a poem that tries harder to be highly poetic, with elevated diction, than others in this volume or Silverstein's other poetry for children. There is one repeated line in the poem: "We shall walk with a walk that is measured and slow," is more lyrical and formal than Silverstein's typical lines of poetry. The archaic "shall" and the repetition of the word "walk," here illustrating polyptoton, or using the same word in two different grammatical forms, as both noun and verb, suggest a self-conscious attempt to sound poetic and dignified. The walk "is measured and slow," suggesting a dignified pace, like a funeral or wedding march, a pace not usually associated with children but one that is purposive, deliberate, and relentless. The whole line sounds like a quotation from another, older, perhaps more famous line of poetry. Its anapestic tetrameter, which usually gives energetic flow to a poetic line, is undercut by the haunting, reminiscent content, which suggests not a waltz but a slow procession or search. Perhaps the line recalls for the more experienced reader the 23rd Psalm, "though I walk through the valley of the shadow of death," or perhaps a line from Poe, whose poetry is also solemn and anapestic.

Silverstein's line also recalls many other poems in which the poet invites the reader into a private world that both will share. Though the exact recollection of the line here cannot be definitely pinned down, Silverstein's effort is clearly to recall for the experienced reader an older, more formal kind of poetry. The diction of "measured and slow," located in a subordinate clause, suggests a way of speaking that is deliberate, not spontaneous, and perhaps even narrative rather than common speech, which Silverstein elsewhere imitates in his poetry. Perhaps it is this different voice that makes the poem less successful as well. Here the subordinate rather than the coordinate grammatical structure and the line's content are both less childlike and more adult, perhaps even elderly. The poem, with its repetitions, formal stanza structure, and careful rhyming, imitates and supports the slow pace of the walk.

The title of both poem and volume succeeds well in suggesting a place uncharted, even uncivilized, where adventure and exploration may take place much as it did for the famous explorers of the Renaissance, who ventured beyond the known, mapped world into the New World. In this way, the title is particularly American, celebrating American initiative and innovation. In the poem, Silverstein celebrates the escape made possible by children and their imaginations and by poetry. By suggesting that the volume's contents are located beyond the boundaries of the commonly accepted and socially controlled, Silverstein's title bodies forth two of the volume's most common themes: the value of outlandish, creative imagination and of the topics that children entertain while imagining, and the undesirability of socially limited behavior. Overall, Silverstein celebrates American children's ability to think for themselves, to find their own new territories and thereby invent new worlds and visions.

Themes and Topics

The theme of children's ability to create magic, to reconstruct the world in a more enjoyable form, is picked up as early as the second and third poems in the volume. Continuing the theme of the opening poem, "Invitation," which invites the child to exercise his imagination, the second poem, "The Acrobats" (10), shows three children swinging from a trapeze, the first hanging on by his nose, the second hanging from the knees of the first, who dangles the third from her toes. The poem is as vertical as the picture's arrangement of the characters. The third character, the poem's ostensible speaker, looks out at the viewer with widespread arms; there is considerable flair and pleasure in his free-flying swing, yet anxiety is visible in his face because he can imagine his peril. He is imaginatively able to contemplate the possibility that the acrobat on top might sneeze. Here imagination can help create a child's wish to accomplish what a circus character might and at the same time create a joke: the poem's final line is level with the anxiety-ridden figure's face. The technique here, the closing punch line that gives order and meaning to the whole poem, is typical of Silverstein; the point is a good joke, one made more comfortable because it exists only in the imagination. The acrobats are only imagined and not real, and no one is in real danger.

Facing this page, without illustration, is the poem "Magic" (11), which echoes the line in "Invitation" about welcoming the "magic bean buyer," a child like Jack, who by luck and perhaps with untaught wisdom, purchases the first cause of his happy ending. Magic for Silverstein is a product of imagination, a gift that children have and will use to good effect if they are adequately encouraged. Silverstein stands as one of the few authors and poets in children's literature who encourages such use of imagination, even though the final effects may be comically disastrous. In "Magic" the voice is that of a child, who envies a catalog of all sorts of magical creatures his friends have met: "leprechaun," "troll," "witches," "goblins," "mermaid," and "elf." All the speaker's friends seem to have put forth no effort to make acquaintance with these characters of myth and story, but the child at the end laments that "I've had to make myself" all the magic he or she has ever come in contact with. The final line, somewhat world weary, is an implied complaint that all the other children have more interesting, easier lives. Yet throughout the volume, Silverstein points to the satisfactions of inventing one's own magic. The glibness of the catalog, the coordinate structure of the list of other children and the creatures they have met, suggest that they may be lying about their fantasy encounters. If they must lie to appear to be such interesting, captivating people, perhaps that is what the speaker should do to enliven his or her life. Making magic by telling stories and using the imagination is one of the highest values this book celebrates.

Weird People, Especially Adults

Some of Silverstein's most remarkable and memorable poems in *Where the Sidewalk Ends* concern outlandish individuals, children and adults with names and peculiar habits that get them into trouble. They are the poems that Donald Hall has most frequently anthologized in *The Oxford Book of Children's Verse in America*.[4] An anthologizer who seeks to array the wide range of children's poetry in the United States, Hall places Silverstein in the tradition of the tall-tale teller who tells exaggerated, humorous stories about children, and sometimes about adults, who, at least initially, seem to be real. From *Sidewalk*, Hall includes "The Dirtiest Man in the World," "Jimmy Jet and His TV Set," and "Sarah Cynthia Sylvia Stout Would Not Take the Garbage Out," and only one poem, "One Inch Tall," about something other than a peculiar individual. Although Hall might have made other choices, from among poems with other themes and foci, he finds Silverstein's strength in the unusual. Even the one poem chosen from *Attic* is about a peculiar individual: the main character of "Clarence" loves television commercials so much that, encouraged by one advertisement, he actually purchases a new set of parents. But more on Clarence's situation in the next chapter.

Myra Cohn Livingston points to these weird poems as evidence of Silverstein's subtle attempts to moralize in *Sidewalk*.[5] "Jimmy Jet and His TV Set" (28–29) literalizes parents' hypothetical threat that if children watch too much television they will turn into one, which is what happens to Jimmy. He grows an electrical cord, knobs for tuning, and antennae for better reception. Although the moral is evident, that too much television viewing is transforming, the whole story is so humorously extreme that it is difficult to see how any child would take it seriously enough to glean any moral value from it. Jimmy may be obsessive and weird, but any adult who thinks that children will take the threat of turning into a TV set seriously is even weirder.

Likewise, Milford Dupree's punishment in "With His Mouth Full of Food" (128) is equally unbelievable. He talks with his mouth full of food until it is glued shut. Melinda Mae in "Melinda Mae"(154–57), rashly promising to eat an entire whale, takes two two-paged spreads and 89 years to do so. The immense and wonderful carcass remaining at the table after the old lady Melinda is done and the extreme passage of time make it difficult to take any moral about keeping promises seriously. Benjamin Bunn (104) cannot undress or attend to his bathroom functions because his buttons are stuck. Once again, it is hard to take seriously the idea that a child may become a social outcast because he or she refuses to change clothes often enough to suit an adult.

In each case, the child character's actions are so extreme as to be humorous. It is difficult to take the lessons they seem to present as serious didactic intent because each child is simply a caricature of his or her bad habit. The situations are so out of hand and the character so monomaniacal in pursuing the bad habit that child readers are more likely to take away the situation's humor than its lesson. In these poems, Silverstein follows the tradition of Lear's limerick, in which people of single oddball characteristics are frozen into a tight rhyme scheme, and of Heinrich Hoffman's nineteenth-century *Struwwelpeter* (1845), which contains situations so grotesque that their examples are laughable. Ogden Nash's peculiar children in *Custard and Company* (1936) bear a close resemblance to Silverstein's peculiars. Silverstein follows the didactic tradition to mock it and to generate humor rather than to preach directly.

One of the book's most potent and continuous themes is criticism of adults and their injunctions. It is in his siding with children and their interests against adults and their definitions of propriety that Silverstein reaches his zenith of credibility. He speaks of what children think about but dare not say in adult company. The choice of topics shows his insight into late-twentieth-century children's lives. He articulates for them their unspoken pleasures in bodily functions, such as spitting, controlled belching, nose-picking, and thumb-sucking; their confusion and consternation about etiquette; their dislike of school; and their pleasure, however fleeting, in holidays. He even deals frankly, though humorously, with sibling rivalry and fear of the dark, and he grants wish-fulfillment to those who hate dentists by having one done in by a crocodile. By creating the voice of a sympathetic, childlike adult and by his pervasive use of humor, Silverstein convinces child readers that he is a trustworthy, accurate spokesman for their point of view and thereby grants legitimacy to the joys and problems of child life that elsewhere are treated patronizingly or trivialized. Silverstein maintains a stance guaranteed to point out the weirdness of adults while distancing his own adult self from them.

The most potent criticism of adults in the book appears in a poem titled "Listen to the Mustn'ts" (27). The child listener is at first commanded to listen to all the words that most characterize adult speech directed at children. These words appear in full capitals to emphasize their absolute, rather than comparative, grammatical construction and thus their power: "MUSTN'TS," "DON'TS," "SHOULDN'TS," "IMPOSSIBLES," "WON'TS," "NEVER HAVES." These words' overwhelmingly negative, prohibitive tone accurately reflects children's perceptions of adults' attitudes toward them and what they want to do. At the poem's opening, the voice echoes the condescending, lecturing tone of adults when they assume superior knowledge and power over children. After his list of power words, however, Silverstein takes a more congenial, intimate, and encouraging stance toward the child: "Then listen close to me— / Anything can happen, child, / ANYTHING can be." The full capitalization of "ANYTHING" stands out as representing Silverstein's point of view about children and what they can and may do. It is a powerful, equal antidote to the long list of prohibitions that precede it. The final line suggests that children follow their imaginations and impulses and be creative, even defiant, in the face of other prohibitions. Once again, Silverstein picks up the themes of the possibilities of life and the power of the imagination, as echoed in the book's first and last poems. He dignifies children's abilities rather than curbs them, a sure way to guarantee children's trust in his voice and poetry.

The poem is unillustrated, except for a small round stone, thrown by Joey Joey from the preceding page. Though the stone serves to unify the graphic design on the two pages, it seems symbolic on this page. It appears about to drop flat on the poem below, a metaphor for flattening either adult prohibitions or the child being harangued by them. Fortunately, Silverstein interprets the illustration's meaning in the last line—it's the adults who get the stone dropped on them. On the previous page Joey has thrown a stone at the sun and brought down eternal night. Although this would appear a tragic situation for humanity, Silverstein immediately counters with a poem of ultimate encouragement for such efforts; after all, it is clear every day that Joey succeeded not in reality but only in imagination, and his effort is heroic, if perhaps thoughtlessly childish.

In the poem "I'm Making a List" (37), Silverstein further criticizes "all the people," especially adults, for all the words they make children use to be polite. The poem is a fairly comprehensive list of all the mannerly short phrases adults try to teach children to use in order to make them acceptably mannered and civilized. The problem is that manners are an artificial construct. Their purpose is to provide social lubrication in order to avoid unpleasantness, or worse, to make social situations easier. But these purposes are not always clear to children, who see manners as unimportant impositions of adult will that force children to behave in ways that seem to them arbitrary and unnatural rather than helpful. Even after an explanation of why one uses these common phrases, politeness may not make sense.

The list, organized vertically with minimal punctuation, is designed to rhyme the word "you" and to provide a terminal rhyme with "May I?" and "Goodbye." Certainly using these phrases would help any child to appear considerate and well behaved, especially when said sincerely and used appropriately. The trouble is that these words are supposed to reform one's feelings and morality, to transform one from a little savage into the representative of all that is beautiful and good in humanity. The purpose of manners is not just superficial change but rather to conjure up in the child "goodness and kindness and gentleness, / sweetness and rightness." In other words, proper mastery of these phrases makes one into a mild-mannered, ideal child, at least from a conventional adult's point of view.

The punch line appears at the end: "If you know some that I've forgot, / please stick them in your eye!" The rudeness of this sentiment is not at all camouflaged by the word "please." But rudeness aside, it is an accurate assessment of a child's sense of manners—all form, with little substance. One has only to look at the mannerly phrases that Silverstein cites to understand their vacuity. After all, when one asks, "How are you?" one usually does not expect a fully expressed and considered answer. And clearly it is only in God's power to bless the sneezer. The phrase has been torn loose from its original meaning and is used in a much more trivial way. And children are frequently encouraged to say "hello" and to demonstrate friendliness even when they are shy or uncomfortable in the presence of someone unfamiliar or unwelcome. The list of proper behaviors and the words that go with them are troublesome to children. Expecting sincere behavior and adding more items to the list are simply unwanted intrusions to the already overloaded child. The humor, the poem's obvious contradiction, and the deflation of adult expectations in the final line make this poem a success with its intended audience, children, though it perhaps raised the hackles of its early audience of adults.

Body Functions and Other Offenses, the Veneer of Civilization

Some of the rules of etiquette do have a purpose; Milford Dupree, in "With His Mouth Full of Food" (128), insists on talking with his mouth full and offends his entire society. But it is not occasional lapses in table manners that cause his lips to become glued together at the end; it is his unwillingness to mend his ways even in front of those who correct him, his parents. The verb that indicates Milford's incorrigibility most offensively is "poo-poo'd," a word that, said aloud, would be likely to spread chewed food all over the reader, if only in his imagination. Silverstein repeats the verb in order to make the most of this gross image and gross disregard for others; "And all they advised him he simply poo-poo'd, / He poo-poo'd with his mouth full of food." Though the word is archaic and is associated with baby talk about excrement, it is particularly effective here. The next couplet describes the gluing of Milford's lips. The last line describes his resolution to reform, although his change of heart arrives too late to permit him to speak clearly. This is what he sounds like with his lips sealed: "I wuntuk win mny marf furu foog," a wonderfully accurate imitation of what "I won't talk with my mouth full of food" sounds like with labial distortion. It is not simple manners and Milford's defiance that make him weird, however. It is his obsessive pursuit of the gross that offends even a tolerant child reader, who might also find humor in the situation. Even Milford's parents seem sympathetic by contrast. Too far is too far, even in a Silverstein poem.

Facing Milford's story is "My Hobby" (129), a poem that celebrates the joys of spitting. Though spitting is offensive, it is amusing, especially when one does it "from the twenty-sixth floor," using targets below to judge one's success. The targets that the narrator uses are designed to make the spittle more obvious and offensive: hats and heads and "white Persian cats," who are averse to liquids of any kind on their fur and who will sport the spittle as a blight on their coats. Spitting from a distance, especially anonymously, is nearly as effective in its offensiveness as spitting in someone's face. Perhaps it is more effective because one can choose victims randomly rather than having to find a reason to be offended. The narrator's pose at the end—"As I smile as I sit, / As I spit from the twenty-sixth floor"—suggests a sly, smug superiority, underscored by his lofty height above the street as well as by his anonymity among his victims. The insulting, unpleasant hobby of spitting is celebrated here, and children, who take pride and interest in the products of their bodies as well as in breaking the rules with impunity, will find as much pleasure in the poem as the speaker does. It confronts a topic and behavior that is so far out of the range of adult propriety that it is unexplained and unmentioned except as an utter prohibition. Here the child narrator avoids weirdness by indulging in spitting as a hobby, not an obsession. The joys of thumb-sucking are celebrated in "Thumbs" (68). "Rudy Felsh" (134) is a champion belcher whom the speaker prays will share his wisdom with him.

In other poems, Silverstein pokes fun at adult prescriptions, proscriptions, and instructions to children. The most offensive and reckless of these poems is "Stone Telling" (147), which answers the question of the first line, "How do we tell if a window is open?" The solution is to toss a rock through it and wait for the noise. The narrator's experimental bent in trying more than one window, the compulsion to move from the first window to the second, echoes children's sometimes destructive behavior in following a logical path or in following instructions to the letter, if not the spirit, of the law. No one capable of reading the poem will be fooled into believing that Silverstein's instructions are anything more than humorous. But sometimes adults insist that, against common sense, children follow rules that are equally confusing and likely to be destructive. Such rules must make about as much sense to children as this particular rule. The poem is almost not a poem, as it is set in short lines but without rhyme or much apparent meter. The conversational tone here is potent, since Silverstein is at once mocking adults and imitating their patronizing tones of address to make his point.

Elsewhere Silverstein celebrates what it would be like to live without adult strictures and other grown-up weirdness, as in "Tree House" (79). The freedom, secrecy, and perspective from on high are certainly enough to make living in a tree house desirable. But the contrast with "a street house, a neat house, / Be sure and wipe your feet house" is enough to cinch the argument. Neatness and confinement close to the ground have no appeal in Silverstein's world.

Silverstein's ultimate comment on manners versus nature appears in the poem "Ma and God" (119), in which he contrasts human law with divine purpose. What seems natural to a child—eating, picking the nose, going gloveless, having dirty, God-created fingers, playing in puddles and the rain, making odd noises, even with trash-can lids, which Silverstein's narrator insists are "God-given" for exactly that purpose— all offend Ma. She says that she expects her children to eat their vegetables, but "God gave us tasteys for maple ice cream." As is typical of Silverstein, the punch line appears at the final line: "Either Ma's wrong or else God is." Ma here is an enforcer of unnaturalness and a killjoy. At every turn, she contradicts what the child in the poem finds natural. God, on the other hand, is supposed to be supportive of whatever the child wants to do, at least according to Silverstein's faith. Certainly the child here thinks that God is in favor of enjoying the world and of using one's body. The answer to the quandary at the end of the poem is clear. God and the child are on the side of right; Ma can go to hell or anyplace else with all her phony rules.

In considering the history of children's poetry, it is difficult to recall a poem in which God is treated so intimately or a mother with such devastating, though humorous, criticism. This mother does nothing dramatically wrong; she simply seeks to inculcate some superficial manners and the veneer of civilization on the child narrator. God is an ally, on the side of the obvious and the natural—use your fingers to eat and try for all the ice cream you can get. Ma is at a rhetorical disadvantage here, especially given the questionable logic about the purpose of God's gifts of fingers and appetites. But she definitely loses this argument, and there's not much she can do to redeem herself. In this poem, eating is an act of defiance, of Ma and all the rules she represents.

This particular poem echoes a theme of anarchy and disregard for societal conventions that appears more frequently in Silverstein's adult works. But the poem's message contrasts with its form. It is written in ballad stanza with precise rhymes, except at the end, where "bodies" rhymes with "God is." The contrast of God with Ma is consistently patterned throughout the poem, giving the reader a reliable expectation of what will come next. Even though Silverstein believes in breaking societal rules, at least when it comes to manners or social mores, he obeys rules with reasonable precision when it comes to writing poetry. None of his verse is experimental in form; only its content questions and pushes boundaries.

Silverstein's most potent vengeance against adults is wrought on dentists in "The Crocodile's Toothache" (66–67). The glee, the reckless disregard for pain, and the sadistic abandonment with which the dentist extracts one tooth after another from the crocodile's mouth mirrors children's ideas about why dentists pull teeth and cause pain—simply because they find perverse pleasure in doing so, not because the procedure is medically necessary. The dentist's excuse, "But what's one crocodile's tooth, more or less?," is echoed in the crocodile's excuse for eating him in retaliation: "But what's one dentist, more or less?" Dentists are expendable as far as many children are concerned and deserve whatever summary end awaits sadists. Adults' belittling of children's distress and adults' lack of sympathy for children's seemingly small mishaps mark a divide between children and adults that Silverstein celebrates rather than crosses.

The poem "Traffic Light" (121) describes what happens when people, especially adults, obey the rules to the extent that they deny common sense: they are frozen in senseless postures of obedience. Silverstein tells the story here of a traffic light that never turns green. After some complaining and honking of horns, the situation continues without change, and days pass into weeks and months. Yet the drivers still sit "[t]widdlin' their thumbs till the changin' comes / The way good people should." The "should" here is a dead giveaway to Silverstein's attitude: the modal is a directive that Silverstein never uses seriously. The people at the end of the poem are still stuck at the corner, "[w]ith the very same smile on their very same face . . . in the very same place." Clearly some daring is in order here.

Poetry of Perspective

It is in showing children another perspective on some piece of wisdom or common occurrence that Silverstein seeks to widen their understanding of the world. One poem, entitled "Point of View" (98), asks the child to consider what eating dinner is like "[f]rom the dinner's point of view." Silverstein does not elaborate about how the food, mostly livestock, feels about being eaten, relying instead on the issue's evocative power and the child listener's innate ability to consider another perspective once its existence is known. Silverstein brings up the same issues about changes in perspective elsewhere, as in "Early Bird" (30), which considers what the sleeping habits of the worm should be if the early bird is an early riser: "sleep late." It is usually the underdog who gets the sympathy in Silverstein's poems. Since children so frequently find themselves in that role, it is not difficult to see the instant appeal of such stories for them.

One of the subcategories of poetry of perspective in this volume is poetry that comments on other literature for children, as foreshadowed by the "magic bean buyer" reference in the volume's first poem, "Invitation." In each case, Silverstein plays out a familiar character or situation from a different perspective or considers a possibility that the original story ignores. One of Silverstein's most haunting poems, and for modern children the least familiar and therefore the least accessible, is "The One Who Stayed" (153), about the child in Robert Browning's "Pied Piper of Hamelin" who is left behind while all the other children are piped away into the mountain's cleft.[6] Most children may know the title and perhaps the main story line of Browning's poem, but few will be familiar enough with the poem to remember the one child who is left behind. This child is a cripple, one who does not move fast enough to keep up with the crowd and who therefore does not get to the magic opening in the mountain before the piper closes it, all the other children having entered before him. This child is a perpetual reminder to the citizens of Hamelin of all the other children who have been lost. His disability makes his presence all the more pitiful and pathetic. It is from him that the reader has the description of the vision that the piper's song promises to the children in order to lure them on:

> a joyous land . . .
> Where waters gushed and fruit-trees grew
> And flowers put forth a fairer hue,
> And everything was strange and new;
> The sparrows were brighter than peacocks here,
> And their dogs outran our fallow deer,
> And honey-bees had lost their stings,
> And horses were born with eagles' wings;
> And just as I became assured

My lame foot would be speedily cured,
The music stopped and I stood still.

The picture presented here is one of Edenic paradise, where things are better than in real life; the promise of a miraculous healing recalls some of the miracles that Christ performs in the gospels, making the promise of an ideal locus even more powerful. Instead of joining his playmates in healthy, joyous play for the first time in his life, the lame boy is left behind to limp through life by himself, the object of pity in his community and a constant reminder of their loss.

"The One Who Stayed" is written from the boy's point of view. The boy's motivation for remaining behind is totally different than that of the boy in Browning's poem. Here he remains because "I was afraid to follow." The boy is not so much left out as willfully choosing his own isolation because he lacks courage and fears risk. This poem picks up the theme of bravery, perhaps even a certain degree of recklessness, as necessary to having a full, interesting life, at least to Silverstein's way of thinking. The boy lets the parade of other children following the piper to a new and better life pass him willingly. This procession even includes "little crippled Bailey," on whom Silverstein displaces the disability in Browning's poem; little Bailey, in spite of his limitations, manages to make it into the mountain. The boy left behind in Silverstein's poem even chooses to abandon other children in his family, who include "brother Rob" and "Cousin Claire." The boy has models whom he might have followed; instead, "I stayed home unheedin' " the piper's music, not because he cannot hear its allure but by deliberate choice and lack of will. Elsewhere in the poem, Silverstein uses unusual, potent diction to describe the boy's father's attitude toward his predicament: "My papa says that I was blest / For if that music found me, I'd be witch-cast like all the rest." Both "blest" and "witch-cast" have associations with religious intervention in human life, the former with a heavenly, positive effect, the latter with a negative, satanic result. The children's destination " 'Cross the hills to God knows where," a line repeated in the poem, suggests that their end is not only unknowable but also providential.

The first appearance of the piper as "that sad stranger" signals this poem's melancholy mood, which is further emphasized by a later line, "This town grows old around me," which suggests the regret and aging effect of the children's absence, hastened by sadness, as well as the child's isolation as the only youth. Altogether, the effect of the elevated diction in this poem, the use of assonance and consonance as devices that suggest repetitious refrains and the regretful quality of Hamelin town's experiences, and the invocation of supernatural forces render the final effect moving and haunting.

The poem is a pathetic emotional experience for the reader familiar with Browning's story. But for the reader who does not know it, who cannot make the connection between the line "piped away the kiddies" and the pied piper, the poem is considerably less effective. "The One Who Stayed" is not a narrative, since the events of Browning's story are not retold except as they are useful in describing the one remaining child's experiences. So the import of the events is not available to this less knowledgeable reader. Given that Silverstein's poem is not narrative, it is therefore dependent on diction and poetic device for its effectiveness. It is difficult to see how the poem would work for a less knowledgeable reader. It is hardly humorous and seems unlikely to move a child reader, though it could certainly do so if it were read in conjunction with Browning's poem. As an exercise in shifting points of view in order to understand the full import of events, reading the two poems together can be an effective learning device. But Silverstein's goal is not to provide material for classroom use. And this poem in isolation is hardly likely to lure children to enjoy his other poetry, especially since it has so few of the humorous and subversive elements that Silverstein's other poems provide so amply.

Another, less complicated example of Silverstein borrowing from older literature for children is "Alice" (112), a six-line poem that refers to Alice's experiences in Wonderland of drinking from a bottle and eating a cake whose contents are unknown, with the result that she changes heights dramatically. Alice's willingness to experiment with these substances and therefore to experience unpredictable change is contrasted with Silverstein's idea of what more pedestrian people are like: "And so she changed, while other folks / Never tried nothin' at all." Though Alice's adventures do not begin with the "Eat Me, Drink Me" experimentation in Lewis Carroll's book, the scene is a memorable one that does lead her to some interesting complications. In the book, she does not eat and drink the substances without considering that they may be dangerous. In fact, she looks for the skull-and-crossbones warning on the label that would indicate poison. Finding none, she consumes carefully, and gradually learns, especially when she eats and then shrinks away to almost nothing, to control her size and her experience by her consumption. In this shape-changing, she experiences some of the changes in perspective that children frequently imagine: what it would be like to be larger, even gigantic, and what it would be like to be so small as not to exist.

Alice's willingness to undertake the adventure, to change, is contrasted in Silverstein's poem with those who are too timid or perhaps simply too complacent to try anything new. Getting inside Alice and understanding her experience from her point of view certainly gives a new perspective to what happens to her in the book, which sometimes seems chaotic and vengeful. And yet seen from another perspective, she is enlarged and rewarded by her willingness to enter into the adventure with body and soul. The appeal of "Alice" is that it is short and the moral is clear, praising children's adventuresomeness as well as criticizing adult indifference and timidity. It is a gem in brevity that, although providing little of the humor most children enjoy in poetry, still delivers, in easy fashion, a message of which they will approve.

In the poem, Silverstein picks up the themes of expanding experiences by risk taking and of diminishing satisfaction with stasis and complacency. For children, change is a way of life; they grow and outgrow experiences and can be frequently bored by that which was just recently new and exciting. Not easily contented for long, their minds and bodies reach out for the new and novel. In this poem and throughout the volume Silverstein both dignifies and praises this restless searching and shows new ways to occupy the mind and be creative.

Silverstein's most effective borrowing from another work for children is the poem "The Little Blue Engine" (158), which provides an antidote to the saccharine sweetness of *The Little Engine That Could*, a picture book retold by Watty Piper, illustrated by George and Doris Hauman.[7] The little blue engine is the name of the successful locomotive in Piper's story. In spite of its age, the story is a well-known one that urges children to keep trying and to encourage themselves as they proceed against the odds. The familiar refrain "I think I can—I think I can—I think I can" has been used as a virtual weapon by adults to urge children on and forms the basis for a singularly American assumption about life, that effort will always succeed. In an earlier time, this adage might have been more true than it is now. Certainly for those victims of racism, sexism, and ethnic discrimination, effort has not been rewarded, but those marginalized voices have been successfully suppressed in literature and in daily life until comparatively recently in the history of children's literature.

Silverstein is up to the task of challenging this ubiquitous assumption about the success of effort. The title of the poem for a short time disguises the identity of the engine, since it is more popularly referred to by the title of Piper's book. That Silverstein presents no illustration with the poem further disguises the train's identity, since it is through the pictures that the engine is most readily identified by young readers and viewers. But the identifying tag line is repeated at the end of the first four stanzas of Silverstein's poem: "I think I can, I think I can, I think I can." Silverstein lets the engine proceed up a long, steep hill, starting with little internal energy and will, moving might and main till he nears the top, until "[h]e was almost there, when CRASH! SMASH! BASH! / He slid down and mashed into engine hash." The repeated internal rhyming, the onomatopoeic effect of the words, and the rapidity of the line, as well as the tension building over four stanzas to this couplet, provide much humor and a kind of relief.

The narrator intrudes at the end of the story, like Aesop, and gives the moral: "If the track is tough and the hill is rough, / THINKING you can just ain't enough!" Although what is needed to succeed is not clearly spelled out, Silverstein's alternative ending accurately reflects that most children's exertions come to naught in at least some cases. The force of positive thinking has long been hailed as salutary by various popular philosophers in the United States. Silverstein provides a more realistic assessment of what clean thinking and persistent effort can achieve, a more honest perspective for children who have been harangued about trying harder. In doing so, he gives validity to children's experiences, provides some humor, which only adds to his credibility among a child readership, pokes fun at other, didactic literature for children, and finally debunks adult authority.

In his use of older literature for children as subjects for his poetry, Silverstein is hardly derivative or imitative but again, subversive and deliberately varied in perspective. He most frequently uses this older literature as a basis for his own perhaps skewed view of the subject. This consistent pattern of shifts in perspective is one that children become more capable of considering as they reach their teens. Being able to recognize shifts in perspective is a developmental stage that Silverstein anticipates and rightly sees as a method of enlarging perception as well as of providing humor. His presentation of these alternate viewpoints demonstrates for children alternate modes of thinking that will both challenge and provide interesting, creative avenues. From a different perspective, suddenly even the familiar becomes new.

One particularly puzzling poem that also seems to borrow from older literature in order to subvert it, "Santa and the Reindeer" (90–91), fails miserably and spectacularly. Silverstein attempts to subvert the unexpected ending but succeeds only in frustrating the reader. The poem, which appears in the center of the book, picks up a theme of holiday poems. "I Must Remember" (14) and "The Fourth" (15), about the Fourth of July, poems that are paired on a two-page spread, express children's experiences of holidays. "I Must Remember" talks about all the foods associated with various holidays and even with days of the week— "Fish on Friday," for example. The protruding belly of the silly person who eats all the foods at the same time is the inspiration for the title. "The Fourth" is a short vertical poem about the noises of the Fourth of July. "Point of View" (98), which follows "Santa," is slightly out of order. It is a provocative poem about Thanksgiving from the turkey's viewpoint—the turkey is "sad and thankless." Valentine's Day has its poem, "Won't You [Be My Valentine]?" (112). The order of poems here is not perfectly consistent with the calendar; is this one of the points of argument between poet and editor that caused the author's sardonic comment to Ursula Nordstrom on his illustrated dedication page? In any case, these holidays are major markers of time for children and are celebrated and promoted not only at home but also at school. A poem about Christmas seems perfectly appropriate in this volume. Another about the same subject, "Merry . . ." (164), is the volume's penultimate. The poem expresses post-Christmas letdown and the distance between the promise of the Christmas season and its practice throughout the year, as noted in the poem's final line about March 25. The Christmas spirit is in fact unique to the season, despite protestations in December that peace on earth and goodwill should last all year long.

So it would seem perfectly appropriate for this varied volume of poetry to have poems about Christmas, at least in its secular manifestation. They are perfectly consistent with other poems in the volume and mark the end of the year: the earliest holiday poem celebrates the Fourth of July, and the last half of the volume includes poems about Valentine's Day and March 25, three months after Christmas, so "Santa," a Christmas Eve poem, is well positioned. The Santa poem also takes up subject matter of some renown in poetry for children: Santa and his reindeer are also the subject of Clement Clark Moore's "A Visit from St. Nicholas" (1823), one of the best-known and most popular poems for children. Santa, one of the most universally recognized and revered heroes of childhood, is always fair and, as far as most children know, always generous. Consistent with Silverstein's inversion of perspective, such as in "Point of View," about the Thanksgiving turkey's feelings about Christmas, this poem picks up on the feelings of one of the reindeer. Thus the poem is all set up for success, either as a wonderful celebration of Christmas or as a great, awful bad joke. Unfortunately, it is neither one.

The reindeer's identity is imbedded in the poem; one has to know all eight of the reindeers' names from Moore's poem in order to be able to figure out which reindeer this is—either Dasher or Vixen, the only two Santa does not call forth in the Silverstein poem. The possibility that the reindeer is Rudolph seems remote, given that it has an ordinary nose in the illustration and given its temerity; Rudolph is all deference and humility, whereas this one is insistent and stubborn, like a dasher or a vixen. Whereas the other reindeer respond to Santa's call, this one stands his ground and asks the old elf, "Oh what do you have for me?" The question confounds Santa; he has "games and toys for girls and boys," which hardly answers the reindeer's question, so he repeats it. Santa grows impatient and distraught; Christmas is upon them and they must leave.

The joke comes when Santa reaches into his beard, pulls out a flea, and puts it into the reindeer's ear, to which the beast responds, "For me? Oh gee!" and takes off. Santa's purpose is accomplished, but is the reindeer's? Is he pleased with the gift or tormented? And in bestowing this gift, Santa reveals himself as being less than the bright, clean, jolly old elf. He is full of impatience and fleas. Silverstein's last couplet in this otherwise well-crafted series of quatrains further confounds the poem's meaning: "And the moral of this yuletide tale / You know as well as me." A series of possible aphorisms comes to mind: ask and you will receive; if you're good, Santa will remember you; you get what you deserve; a little kindness goes a long way; good things come in small packages; it is better to give than to receive; what goes around comes around. Unfortunately, none of these adages seems quite right, since none acknowledges the obvious hostility between the reindeer and Santa. And none of them accounts for Santa's lack of consideration for the reindeer or for the reindeer's sudden, unexplained, and untimely request for a gift after all the years of unspoken cooperation. Finally, nothing in the poem helps the reader to understand whether the reindeer's "Oh gee!" is an expression of pleasure or of torment; perhaps it is both.

Further clouding the poem's meaning are its illustration and details. The reindeer sees a "falling star"; traditionally, falling stars in literature

and popular lore mean that someone is dying. At the very least, a falling
star is a portent of something of weighty significance. Is the reindeer
here the voice of all those who do not ask for and therefore do not
receive Christmas gifts? Is he the one about to die or at least experience
some kind of unpleasant fate? The detail, rather than clarifying, further
confounds.

The reindeer is also described as speaking in low whispers and standing "as if made of wood." The illustration shows the reverse. The two
characters stand on opposite sides of the gutter in obvious confrontation. The reindeer seems ready to charge Santa, his full rack of antlers
poised for action and his small eyes focused in a glare. Santa looks back
at him in helpless, slump-shouldered confusion. The bags under his eyes
and the droop of the usually cheery pom-pom at the end of his hat make
him look dirty and unsavory, as the flea in his beard suggests he might
be. The illustration does not bear out the reindeer's meek request and
lends to Santa the aura of not quite being in control, although he clearly
is at the end of the poem; in fact, he treats the whole incident with the
reindeer as a brief pause, not the last part of a bad, harried day. The
opposition of reindeer and Santa is clear in the picture, but the attitudes
of the two about the final resolution are not. The ending is subversive
because it is so open to interpretation, whereas the poet points to a
closed, finalized, and moralized ending. Only Silverstein knows what
the poem really means, and he isn't telling. Perhaps the poetry is just
sloppy, but the poet's smug silence about the moral at the end undercuts
the friendly, accessible stance he has taken elsewhere. Other poems in
this volume fail, but none as spectacularly as this one.

Affection and Aggression

Elsewhere, Silverstein honors children's experiences of themselves and
their world by making them subjects of poems, even when they are
behaving unacceptably. He accurately articulates for children what they
have experienced but have not spoken about. In a more acceptable vein,
he celebrates children's experiences of holidays: "the Fourth" of July
(15), which passes in noisy, interrupting spurts until one can sigh with
certain relief that it's over; Valentine's Day, in "Won't You?" (112),
which articulates children's anxiety about finding an appropriate and
available partner on that day; and about several holidays together,
which children experience through their distinctive foods, in "I Must

Remember" (14), in which a boy remembers what the appropriate dishes are for various holidays but proceeds to eat them all at the same time, much to his regret, as his extended waistline in the picture illustrates.

The volume also provides poems about bodies in general, celebrating their pliability and changeability rather than their grossness. Children's bodies are not just offensive, they are glorious as well, always changing, and the sources of confusion. "Ourchestra" celebrates the noises that bodies can make, though one child illustrated next to the poem has a nose shaped like a clarinet and another has a stomach large enough to function well as a drum. "The Loser" (25) demonstrates what it would be like if one could actually lose one's head; "Rain" (40) entertains the possibility of the falling water penetrating the head and sloshing around in the brain. As Livingston has noted, throughout the book heads are a featured body part because of their capacity to identify people, because of their function as repositories of imagination and thinking, and because of the revenge made possible by eating.[8] The dentist consumed by the crocodile is but one example of the latter. Similarly, a baby sibling is eaten up, to the mild consternation of observers in "Dreadful" (141). The sibling speaker's crime is revealed only in the last line, by an unintended "(burp)." The "Boa Constrictor" (44–45) eats the speaker of the poem from foot to head in painfully detailed stages. The ultimate eater is "Hungry Mungry" (160–61), who consumes the whole world, then, because of his uncontrollable appetite, starts eating himself until his teeth are the only objects left in the whole universe.

Eating usually signifies aggression in this book, but it can also be a source of great pleasure. This is not to say that eating for children is like sex for adults in literature, as some psychological critics might assert. Certainly adults are as interested in food as children are, and most writers know that sex in a children's book will either get it banned or keep it from being published at all. But eating is a central part of children's lives, and teeth can be a useful weapon for someone without a large repertoire of behaviors or tools to deal with feelings of aggression and powerlessness.

Silverstein's love poems are good places to examine what his feelings about humanity are. One poem, "Love" (95), is a simple two-couplet stanza explaining the illustration, in which one child holds up a poster sign with a giant V on it. The narrator explains that the children who were to hold up the other letters that spell "love" are, for various reasons, absent, and "I'm all of love that could make it today." Although the poem avoids sloppy sentimentality, some readers may feel that the lone child needs to be reassured that the love he offers is sufficient and worthy. After all, his loneliness makes him somewhat pitiful. Silverstein may also be commenting on various fads surrounding the word *love* at the time he was writing. The word, which became a kind of mantra in the sixties, was displayed in such items of popular culture as jewelry, T-shirts, and even a postage stamp. But the critic of such a small poem must be careful not to read anything more than a small joke into it. The other children are missing, but one cannot ascribe to them the motivation of being too busy, preoccupied, or misanthropic; they are simply not present to complete the visual effect of spelling out "love." The poem is a potent comment on children's plans to participate in shows and demonstrations and on the difficulty of coordinating even small numbers of children for public recitals.

In "My Rules" (74), Silverstein is a bit more telling about children's ideas about love. The narcissistic child speaker's requirements for the ideal marriage partner include being a perfect cook, a mender of socks, and a comforter of the partner's mind and body. This sounds like a traditional set of requirements for an ideal wife—that she be submissive, attentive, and domestically all-competent. The list continues and takes a turn toward the dictatorial with the line "and while I rest you must rake up the leaves." The image of someone scurrying around raking while the speaker reclines at ease brings the speaker's actions into view for the first time. The perfect partner has been busily described, but the speaker's attributes, except for his propensity to nap, have been thus far unknown. The list continues, with the mate silently shoveling snow while the speaker does all the talking.

The punch line begins when the speaker is about to list another requirement, at which point he is interrupted by the prospective mate: "And—hey—where are you going?" By this time, most children and adult readers would expect some balking from the hypothetical mate; obviously the speaker is hardly a worthy one to mate with. But the list of requirements can be applied not only to ideal mates but also to ideal children and perhaps to children's expectations of ideal parents as well. Both parents and children sometimes expect too much of each other, and both can become hopelessly self-centered in their demands. Both the perfect child, who is neat, helpful, attentive to chores, and seen but not heard, and the perfect parent, who provides for the child's every need and whim and who does the child's chores without complaint, are described in this list. Though it is a commonplace that children are narcissistic, such a character flaw is not the sole domain of childhood. In this poetic joke, Silverstein is not damning marriage as abuse of one partner by the other or criticizing familial relationships. He does point to the need for mutuality in all intimate relationships in order for them to exist at all. In the poem's progress, from one absolute, self-centered requirement to the next, children can recognize their own demanding behavior and laugh because the list of demands is so relentless and excessive.

The desire for exclusivity in love relationships is criticized directly in "Just Me, Just Me" (152). Though the speaker asserts in the first line that "Sweet Marie, she loves just me," another voice, in alternate lines framed in parentheses, claims Marie's love of Maurice McGhee, Louise Dupree, and the willow tree. In spite of the speaker's growing vehemence about his status as Marie's sole love object, the final couplet brings the speaker up short: "(Poor, poor fool, why can't you see / She can love others and still love thee.)" The immensity of the human capacity for love is affirmed here, as is the noncompetitiveness of loving. The poem verges on corny cliché, but Silverstein avoids such a pitfall in two ways: first, by echoing either the voice of children who wish for the security of such exclusive relationships with parents—"Mom loves me best"—or the voice of childhood sweethearts, who frequently change their minds and partners. Second, he diversifies Marie's other beloveds—a male, a female, a tree—making it clear that this is a poem not about romantic love but about universal love. Thus the poem stays clear of the problematical sentimentality of greeting-card verse.

"The Bagpipe Who Didn't Say No" (132–33) is a poem about the unrequited love of a turtle for a bagpipe. Written in the style of Lear's "Yonghy-Bonghy Bo" and the traditional rhyme "The Spider and the Fly," it sets up the situation of unequals in love, in which one partner continues throughout life stricken by the fact that his beloved does not respond to his overtures, however inappropriate. The turtle is obviously making overtures of love to an inanimate object; the bagpipe's only response is the onomatopoeic "Aooga," which, as the title suggests, is not exactly saying no. The whole poem is framed as a nonsense story, in which realistic details are added to make an incongruous whole: "It was nine o'clock at midnight at a quarter after three." After the turtle has departed, crestfallen, with no affirmation of mutual affection from the bagpipe, the narrator asserts the story's reality by suggesting that the reader verify the facts with the bagpipe: "Just walk up and say, 'Hello, there,' / And politely ask the bagpipe if the story's really so. / I assure you, darling children, that the bagpipe won't say 'No' " because the bagpipe cannot say anything at all. This poem is a comment more on the nature of nonsense than on the nature of love, though Silverstein is certainly examining the complexities of choosing appropriate partners and of the obsessional quality that love can sometimes take on.

Love for parents and adults does not appear in any of the poems. As Alison Lurie notes about *Alice in Wonderland,* an exemplar of subversive literature for children, there are no commendable adults.[9] However, love for siblings is evident in *Sidewalk,* through its reverse: sibling rivalry. "Hat," with its illustration of the stupid younger sibling wearing the toilet plunger on his head, touches on this theme briefly. But "For Sale" (52–53), about the auction of a "crying and spying young sister," expresses the rivalry in vivid language and illustration. The auctioneer and speaker is an older sibling, a brother, as made evident through the illustration. "Crying and spying" are hardly marketable values, though they certainly describe the offenses said sister has committed that have led to such drastic action. Of course, the brother cannot get an opening bid of even a single cent. The resolution of the situation is implied by the final sentence, a question—are there no takers? There is no easy resolution to sibling rivalry, though a sense of humor about it, usually not found during sibling warfare, is helpful. Silverstein tries to inject such a humorous note, at least in the poem's text.

The illustration is another matter. The caricature of the older brother is one of the least flattering in the whole volume. Usually, illustrations are meant to move the story along; characters facing right get the reader to move in that direction and turn the page. The auctioneer brother appears on the left-hand page, facing left, in an antiprogressive, flabby stance. He has a large mouth and a large belly, which his slovenly posture allows to hang out between his T-shirt and belt. His eyes are small, as is his forehead, and his stance is accusatory, one finger pointing down toward the sister, one hand raising a gavel. The gavel actually looks more like a ball-peen hammer, and he handles it as though prepared to do business with a nail rather than with a buyer. His is the first figure the viewer sees in the leftward glance across the page, assuming that the viewer looks at the left-hand portion of the two-page spread before reading the poem on the left-hand page above.

Almost lost in this wide arc across the two pages is the offending sister, who sits like a final punctuation mark at the bottom right of the two-page spread; the right page is void of illustration except for her portrait. She hardly seems the menace that she is advertised to be: in profile, she sits with her back to her brother, a tear dripping from her face, her legs too short to reach the ground from the platform the two share. Her hunched shoulders, the bow holding her long hair, and the fact that she is at the bottom of the page make her seem forlorn, isolated, and smaller and much more pathetic than the brother, who is clearly a brute. She is compact, with a clear face except for the tears; he is large and dominant on his page, his teeth bared and face spotted, usually indicators of dishonorable character. The idea of auctioning off an offending sibling is funny and raucous in the text, but the illustration tells another story, one that reminds a well-read reader of the nearly deadly rivalry between the younger Joseph and his 10 older, unsympathetic brothers in the Old Testament. Silverstein seems willing to give voice to some rather violent feelings in the poem, but not without commenting on the victim's point of view in the last part of the illustration.

"What a Day" (118) voices the prematurely fatigued feelings of an eight-year old, whose "baby brother ran away / And now my tuba will not play." That such events are marked by the understated letdown of the middle-aged tone of voice in the poem's title indicates that these two events are equally oppressive but not calamitous. When the picture reveals the baby brother hiding out in the bell of the tuba, the viewer understands that the older brother probably hasn't tried very hard to find his younger sibling and that the baby is hiding out rather than having run away. Disposal of the young pest seems acceptable here.

War and Race Relations

Silverstein is at his most shocking and most effective in a series of unexpected poems. Of all the topics Silverstein might have chosen for children, war seems the least likely. In fact, children's books that have chosen war as subjects, such as Dr. Seuss's *Butter Battle Book* (1984), have been controversial targets for censors and critics. Given the public debate about the Vietnam conflict at the time *Sidewalk* was published, war, its justification, and its effects were certainly current and available as topics for poetry, though not necessarily poetry for children.

Silverstein takes on the popular conception of war as glorious, rational, and justified in "The Generals" (150–51). Generals Clay and Gore's names have heavy connotative value: generals have feet of clay and their bodies will return to clay; they are not immortal or infallible. Gore is the usual outcome of any battle. The two start out well enough in their debate about continuing a war in which they are both involved. It is not clear whether they fight against each other or as comrades. Their debate is particularly childish; both agree that the war is "silly"; "To kill and die is such a bore." They agree to go to the beach instead of continuing the battle. But even after agreeing to this alternative, they both find reasons not to go but rather to stay and fight. One general has a torn bathing suit; the other is fearful of drowning, though they both agree beforehand about the pleasures of building sand castles. So rather than call off the war, they agree to continue, to the point of mutual self-destruction: "And now, alas! there is no more / Of General Clay or General Gore." Silverstein implies here that the leaders of wars have no justification for what they do and no clear understanding of the damage they perpetrate on others and themselves. Under such leadership as that of Clay and Gore, there is no such thing as an honorable war.

The line drawings for this poem are more detailed than most other illustrations in the book and more closely approximate Silverstein's character studies in such adult books as *Now Here's My Plan* (1960). The generals, foppishly dressed, with medals and decorations hanging, face each other, but with little soldierly smartness. Their faces look besotted and ill-shaven, their postures anything but erect. As leaders and generals, they are clearly not admirable. One holds a revolver, the other a sword, and both pack other war armaments, perhaps bayonets, on their backs. They stand in profile debating on the left-hand page of a two-page spread. On the lower right-hand side of the right page, below the end of the text, all that is left is the revolver and the sword in the sand, like abandoned beach toys, so total is their self-destruction. Silverstein finds nothing of value in these leaders or in the war they conduct; all things pale compared to a day at the beach. War is diminished to a bad alternative to a day of childhood pleasures.

At the time this collection was published, debate still roared in the public sector about the Vietnam War. Silverstein enters this debate, in both text and illustration, on the side of the doves. He also brings the issue, somewhat simplified, of course, to children in such a way that they feel compelled to agree with him. Although other poems in the volume deal with the smaller, though still compelling issues of child life, Silverstein is not shy about taking on the larger political issues of the 1970s and time periods both before and after. Wars continue and children should know about them.

Silverstein also deals with the issue of race relations in two poems, "No Difference" (81) and "Colors" (24). The first poem concludes that all people are alike in the dark, and so the solution for straightening out human relations "[i]s for God to just reach out / And turn off the light!" The assertion that all human beings have equal value in spite of superficial differences settles the issues of race, class, and appearance. This resolution offers children the appealing possibility of a just world in which all earn respect. Children, small and frequently ignored, and all others who have been treated unfairly would find this message particularly appealing.

"Colors" deals more directly with race relations. Although the speaker claims to have skin tones that are "brownish / Pinkish yellowish white," his eye and hair colors encompass even more of the spectrum, and inside he has more colors still. Again, racial differences, especially as judged by skin and hair pigment, seem less definite; most people have most colors in them, so that differences are accommodated rather than differentiated. "Colors" is oblique in dealing with the social issues it implies and can be read as an exercise in coloring with a wide assortment of crayons; "No Difference" confronts the issue more clearly. Silverstein wisely does not illustrate either poem; black and white do not lend themselves to discussions of the range of the palette, and with the lights off, no one sees anything anyway.

Of all the poems in the book, "Hug O' War" (19) is most clearly the signature poem, in its playful, accommodating attitude toward human relations and conflict. The illustration accompanying it, of two small children hugging and looking at the viewer with smiles and tiny dot eyes, is the one chosen for promotional blurbs for *Sidewalk* on dust jackets for other Silverstein books. The drawing's simplicity, the children's obvious affection for each other and for the viewer, and the illustration's smallness, a tidy block like a postage stamp, all stand for the experience of the whole book. This is also the illustration that introduces this book on its own dust jacket and graces the bottom of the title page. The happy relations between children, one a boy and one a girl, the emphasis on their smiles and their encompassing arms, the solidity of their stance, all suggest pleasure and play and none of the less pleasant aspects of life that Silverstein deals with elsewhere.

The title is obviously a play on "tug o' war," which the speaker of the poem says that he or she will not play. Whereas tug o' war is dependent on competition and physical might, a zero-sum game in which one team must lose so the other can win, hug o' war is more inclusive and less dependent on players' skill and physical prowess. Hug o' war is charac-terized by affectionate roughhousing, laughter, and participation by "everyone," a word repeated six times in the short 10-line poem. Players have only to follow their natural inclinations to have fun in order to par-ticipate and succeed, and there are no injunctions about being a good loser or about how well players play the game. The rhyme and meter in this poem are perfect, and the sentiment is difficult to take exception to; Silverstein has written many good poems in this book and elsewhere, but this one comes closest to perfection. He is both celebratory of child-hood pleasure and subversive of adult warfare. Although Silverstein cel-ebrates pleasure, here he is at his most didactic: war is unacceptable.

Overall, Silverstein's view of human relationships is both optimistic and hopelessly depressing. On the one hand, he can celebrate the human capacity for oneness; on the other, he can deplore humans' abuses of each other while positing no counterbalancing hope. It is diffi-cult to pin the author's philosophy on one extreme or the other. Cer-tainly "Hug O' War" and "No Difference" suggest that there is much capacity among human beings to accept and enjoy each other. The array of poems in this volume suggests that life is varied and that emotions shift. The poet represents this range of emotions but does not stand pat at any one point to avoid propagandizing or to admit the reality of the extremes. The poems are arranged throughout the volume in such a way as to present these alternating feelings, with some relief by intervening focus on other topics.

Poems about Poetry and Poetic Techniques

In the poet's tradition, Silverstein reflects on his own writing and includes several poems about poetry, especially those that encourage children to try a hand at it. Quite appropriately, he uses short poems with short lines and easy rhymes to make the poetry appear as easy as possible. Following up on the word "liar" in the opening poem "Invita-tion," he suggests that being a glib, easy liar is one of the essential char-acteristics of making rhyme and poetry. In "Who" (63), the speaker boasts of his many accomplishments, worthy of television and comic book superheroes. At the conclusion, the speaker admits his fabrica-tions: "Who can sit and tell lies all night? / I might!" The ease of the rhyme in this line and throughout—for example, the pronoun *I* with a modal verb—makes for rapid-fire self-confirmation not only in accomplishing the superhuman but also in composing poetry. The poem "Toucan" (92) makes for easy rhyming as well; to rhyme with toucan, one simply finds a subject and adds the verb *can*. Here the subjects all rhyme with *two*, making for spondaic monometer, a short line with only one metrical foot. The poem moves quickly with short lines that end with feminine, falling meter, increasing the humor. The final verse, "Who can write some / More about the toucan? / You can!," makes it easy for the child to take up the challenge and rhyme a few more verses. By making it look easy, Silverstein makes poetry the province of the child and instills confidence in his creative power to write poetry, however simple in technique and effect.

"Enter This Deserted House" (56) invites the reader into a forbidding, decaying house that has no roof or floors, only sunshine and flowers for architecture. The inside is hardly what the reader expects, since it is both haunting and inviting: there are frogs, crickets, bats, owls, gnomes, and goblins, as well as the speaker and the listener: "And my child, I thought you knew / I dwell here . . . and so do you." In this poem, Silverstein celebrates the power of illusion and suggestion; the house should be dark, but one's vision of it can make it sunny and natural. That both speaker and listener live in this house suggests that listeners are capable of scaring themselves voluntarily, for pleasure's sake, with their own imaginations. The poet can change what is frightening into something pleasant and attractive, and so can the child. The power to create, as well as to dispel, resides in both child and poet, and Silverstein invites the reader, as fellow resident of the deserted house, to enter the range of emotion as a part of the experience of the book and of life.

As X. J. Kennedy and Dorothy M. Kennedy have noted, children's poetry remains untouched by the innovations of poetic style that have changed poetry for adults so radically.[10] Children's poetry still relies heavily on rhyme and meter for effect, as does Silverstein's, except that he is markedly less technical than most poets for children. Much of Silverstein's verse appears easy and casual, especially in the repeated dropping of the final *g* in words ending in *-ing*. One can imagine that a poet who comes to written verse from writing rock and roll or blues lyrics is more used to composing and revising out loud than drafting and revising on paper. Certainly that is the case with Silverstein, who in his recordings of these poems frequently breaks into song. In fact, some of the poems collected in *Sidewalk* have been recorded by others, most notably "The Ballad of the Unicorn" (76–77), by the Irish Rovers, and "Boa Constrictor" (45), by Peter, Paul, and Mary.

The casualness of Silverstein's verse is underscored by most poems' short lines, which demand less lengthy considerations of meter, and by some of the nonce words, made to rhyme with an earlier word. For example, in "Wild Boar" (68), "abouth" (about) is made to rhyme with "mouth"; "shore" (sure) rhymes with "boar." The oral quality of these rhymes is a clue to Silverstein's success with his youthful audience. The poems are made to tell aloud, to recite and thereby to provide pleasure, both to reciter and to hearer. The oral nature of children's lore has long been known; here Silverstein crosses the border into written formats. He manages to put into print language that children could imagine themselves using. The high poetical is not in evidence because it is not authentic to children's language experience.

As mentioned previously, the poem's punch line, or final twist, either in the last lines or at the bottom of an illustration, is another of Silverstein's techniques that is not strictly poetical but is still narrative. As befitting a narrative technique, it is most effective in the longer narrative tall tales, such as "True Story" (43), in which the narrator tells a breathless story of wild adventure; the story begins with a cowboy shootout, then progresses to pirate capture, to torture by burning to death, to jungle adventure, and to cannibalism. The tale is told in the first person by the first person, who gallops through the story quickly. The compound sentences have equal, coordinate structures, and all details are equally important. The story is highly improbable, full of narrow escapes from popular life-threatening scenarios, until the end, when the narrator is rescued from the penultimate problem by a flying eagle: "But he dropped me in a boiling lake / A thousand miles wide. / And you'll never guess what I did then— / I DIED." The poem ends with uncharacteristic finality, made more potent because the word "died" finishes a predictable pattern of rhymes throughout the poem, starting in the second line with the word "ride." The joke is on the reader and hearer, since it is obvious that the teller cannot be dead if he is still telling the story in the first person; a second level of irony exists in the poem's title, which also cannot be true. The final and unexpected ending is humorous, as are most of the volume's punch-line endings. Even short poems in the limerick style use this technique, to the same humorous effect. It is the humor that most children remember about the book and comment on.

The long, narrative poems are seldom composed of verses but instead continue as long as four pages, as with "The Flying Boy" (136–39), about a boy with long hair whom the wind catches and spirits away to unknown parts. This poem does not succeed as well as others that are long and less serious because its open, inconclusive ending and purposelessness offset its solemnity. More effective are the long poems "Sarah Cynthia Sylvia Stout Would Not Take the Garbage Out" (70–71) and "Sick" (58–59). The punch-line ending again prevails here, but the real force of these poems is their plethora of imaginative, disgusting detail that the narrators reel off. In Sarah's case, the poem's cautionary nature is undercut by the disgusting details of the garbage she will not take out; the details are so disgusting that I have found it impossible to listen to Silverstein narrate the poem in totality without experiencing nausea. The narrative here deliberately avoids the punch line, which is nonetheless utterly apparent from the illustration. The "awful fate, / That I cannot right now relate / Because the hour is much too late" is that Sarah is buried in the garbage in which both narrator and delighted child hearer have so specifically wallowed. The caution, related in deliberately parental tones, is complete with the requisite "always," the signal of parental stance. The mounds of garbage so lovingly detailed in both narrative and illustration distract from any seriousness that such a tale might have been able to muster. As a cautionary, didactic tale, the poem follows more in the tradition of Hoffman's laughable *Struwwelpeter* than of Isaac Watts.

"Sick" is a compendium of health excuses to avoid school. The excuses range from the trivial, such as a hangnail, to the ominous and unexplainable, such as a broken leg. The list continues, improbably piling symptoms of chicken pox on top of scoliosis, until Peggy Ann McKay, the poem's speaker, realizes that "today is . . . Saturday" and then beats a swift retreat out of bed in the last line: "G'bye, I'm going out to play!" (59). Again, details pile up rapidly, improbably stacked on top of each other in swift, rhyming lines, until the punch line. The technique's success here has been borne out by classroom experience. Teacher James Hemphill decided to have 72 fourth, fifth, and sixth graders vote on their favorite poem of all time after they had studied poetry extensively in class and submitted candidates for the honor. In spite of Hemphill's introduction of the class to poems by other well-known poets for children and in spite of Hemphill's and the children's offers of numerous alternatives, Silverstein was the only poet the children knew by name, and the winner was Peggy Ann McKay and her excuses.[11] The poem's popularity with Hemphill's students is not hard to assess: it lies in Peggy Ann's ability to make up excuses with breathless speed and in reasonably precise verse while still sounding like a child. She rhymes "sprained" with "rains," and "mouth" with "out." But the speed with which she invents does not allow the reader to stop long enough to criticize her or Silverstein's rhyming technique. The final effect is awe at the powers of invention, as provoked into action by a familiar childhood situation.

The poem, in its clear articulation of children's propensity to invent illnesses in order to avoid school, might seem to poke fun at children's transparency. In another poet's hands, the effect might be humor at the child's expense and embarrassment at being revealed as a liar. But in Silverstein's hands, children are sympathetic to both Peggy Ann's attempts to stay home and to her miraculous cure at the end. Silverstein here is himself one of the children, capable of telling lies and giving pleasure therein. Admitting children's faults and exaggerating them to make them absurd and laughable avoids the usual adult stance of using specific examples to demonstrate right behavior by contrast. Indeed, James Hemphill's bravery in presenting the poem to children and thus providing them with a new set of excuses for avoiding school shows his trust in the poem's humor and his willingness to let the humor stand on its own, without intervening to caution the children about following Peggy Ann's example.

The arrangement of *Sidewalk*'s longer poems, which alternate with shorter ones, provides variety and pacing throughout the book. As many as four poems can occupy one two-page spread, as with pages 74 and 75, on which all four poems end with a humorous punch line. The ultimate childhood joke in "Oh Have You Heard," for example, ends with "APRIL FOOL!" (75). Others, such as "The President Has the Measles," are full of possible but unlikely situations. One poem makes ultimate mockery of the cautionary tale; "Warning" (75) points to the perils of picking one's nose, in other times and places a topic that would hardly have been considered appropriate for children's poetry but nonetheless one of those points of etiquette that every child has learned about the hard way. Silverstein posits "a sharp-toothed snail" inside the nose, which bites off fingers. The accompanying illustration shows a surprised person, hair standing straight up on top of his head, eyes opened in utter surprise, as he experiences the pain of this phantom boogeyman who dwells with the boogers.

Elsewhere, the endings are less humorous, lacking punch and punch lines, but perhaps more provocative. A snowman who tries to stay alive until summer in order to experience it becomes a puddle at the end of "The Snowman" (65). The characters in "Ickle Me, Pickle Me, Tickle Me

Too" (116–17) fly off and away to no place in particular, a frequent ending to Silverstein's poems about flying. Simon in "The Garden" (61) lives in an amazing world of jewels, only to find himself longing for "one . . . real . . . peach." Silverstein's more contemplative poems, which frequently investigate the meaning of desire and the purposes of living, signal their questing and ruminating with endings about lack of satisfaction. That he uses his endings, whether humorous or open, to such good effect underscores his philosophy of process and quest as the meaning of life. At the end of each poem, even after the humor of a punch line has died away, the reader is left with the challenge of what comes next. Where is the next subject of interest? Life for Silverstein provides few permanent satisfactions, but there is a lot of fun to be had along the way.

Sometimes even the last line of the poem's text is not the ending. "The Planet of Mars" (93) describes Martians as being much like earthlings, with similar bodies and clothing and "the same heads and same faces," though not in the same locations. It takes the illustration of a human form with the smiling head located on the rump, another butt joke, to ascertain the full meaning here. The location of the head, at the right side of a right-handed page, is typical of Silverstein's illustrations; the viewer frequently reads the picture, with the punch line detail, last. "For Sale" (52) commences with a picture of an auctioneering brother on the far left side of the narrative, on the left page. It is not until the reader/viewer sees the small figure of the crying, round-faced little sister, hopelessly hunched over on the lower right side of the right-hand page, that he sees the poem's full import. Although the older brother's gusto in selling off his bratty sister is humorous, from her point of view, and the poet and illustrator's as well, her brother causes her pain.

Finally, it is the multiplicity of voices that Silverstein brings forth, in full, convincing tonality, that sustains the reader's interest in this volume. Edward Blishen commends Silverstein and Michael Rosen, another poet, for their "desire to celebrate the true raffishness of childhood" but admonishes that such poetry must "stop a long way short of pretending that social unacceptability is the beginning and the end of it," for such poetry "at its worst . . . is probably as bad and as merely fashionable as anything in those older anthologies against which we are reacting."[12] It is certainly true that some of the voices Silverstein uses are clownish and only that. Yet *Sidewalk* is saved from condemnation by Blishen's own admission because there are significant moments of contemplation, of adult encouragement for imagination and risk-taking, of speculation about the motivations of legendary figures and about larger-than-life events. It is unfair to dismiss the wide array of voices as simply gross because that kind of humor predominates, though the rough humor is a major part of the volume's success. But this is not simply a collection of naughty, off-color, offbeat jokes. The book investigates such matters of substance as the nature of obedience, the satisfactions of life, and the nature of desire. Although Silverstein is not the only poet through which children can investigate these matters, he is one of the few who sustains interest in them, precisely because he uses a variety of voices and intersperses the humorous with the serious so that the overall effect is not overpowering in philosophical discussion nor as easily dismissed as rapid-fire jokes.

Techniques of Illustration.

Sidewalk is relentlessly black and white, from dust jacket to final page. Although the illustrational technique of black line drawing in carica-ture, cartoon fashion might pale in comparison with more lavishly illus-trated volumes, the amplitude of white space, without the confusion of a cartoon technique, gives each figure a sense of full value and breathing space. There are no balloons that the figures speak into, no panel frames, few details of background. The attention is concentrated on the figure and the text. Even a cartoon technique can show remarkable vari-ation in the hands of a dedicated, professional cartoonist. To be sure, some of the lines are heavy and some of the outlines hard; others are more sketchy, more suggestive of anxious, frenetic, worrisome move-ment. Some of the illustrations are simple enough to suggest that a child might have drawn them—albeit a particularly talented child, as with "The Land of Happy" (143), which features a smiling round face with a slight wrinkle to the grin. Others are more replete with detail, shading, and intense emotion, as with the illustration for "The Crocodile's Toothache" (66–67), which features a fiendish dentist armed with pliers inside a cavernous crocodile's mouth; the crocodile is ensconced in a dentist's chair, complete with spitting basin and high-powered lamp. The simple flap of skin under the crocodile's eye suggests a tear; the dentist's wild abandon despite the crocodile's menacing teeth and his obvious lack of care about the crocodile's pain accurately depict the underlying theme: that adults do not care about children's pain and that adults' mean-spiritedness will be their own undoing.

Sometimes the illustration is the poem itself, as with "Poem on the Neck of a Running Giraffe" (107), in which the words form the giraffe's neck. And sometimes the conventions of book design comment on the poem. "Afraid of the Dark" (159) is a baby's first-person narration of his fears at bedtime; the baby, who must have the light on, implores the reader at the end of the poem, "So please do not close this book on me," which the reader must do by either turning the page or putting the book away. Finally, the last poem, facing the blank right-hand page, suggests that poetry goes on after the book is over and that the reader is left to his own devices to fill the right page and the rest of life beyond, though not without guidance from the poet. The illustrator makes good use here, and throughout, of the general direction in which readers read an illustration: both before and after reading the text and from lower left to upper right.

Critical Evaluation

There are some notable failures in this collection of poems; some of the serious poems seem to be holdovers from Silverstein's career as a lyricist of rock and country-and-western music, more suitable for adults in their fuzzy, woebegone sentiments than for children. "Poor Angus" (117), with his sentimental dependence on his beloved Catherine, is one such poem; even "The Unicorn" (76–77) works better as a song than it does as a stand-alone poem. "The Long-Haired Boy" (137–39), who is carried away by the wind from a heartless world to heaven knows where, is sentimental and unresolved as well as unrelieved by wit or interesting poetry. "Where the Sidewalk Ends" (64) and "Santa and the Reindeer" (90–91) have endings that point to some kind of meaning, but in "Santa" the effort to figure out the didactic intent is deliberately frustrating, and in "Sidewalk" the ending is vague and sentimental about the value of children's adventurousness and imagination. Elsewhere, as in "Magic" (11), "Mustn'ts" (27), "The One Who Stayed Behind" (153), and even the opening poem, "Invitation" (9), Silverstein's expression of the wondrous possibilities of the human imagination and human striving are much more successfully celebrated. And as will be seen in the next chapter, Silverstein's illustrational skills and the range of emotions and voices of which he is capable improve, as does his ability to design a unified two-page spread, even one that contains more than one poem.

Overall, however, *Sidewalk* is a success and opens the way for the more provocative, more serious, and funnier poems in *Light in the Attic*.

Many of the poems in *Sidewalk* take on subjects that might seem unlikely for poetic consideration, such as Band-Aids, boredom, postholiday letdown, and belching. The range of emotions is wider than in most anthologies for children because Silverstein is willing to entertain the negative feelings that children obviously have but that poets for children and those who teach their poems have denied. These mentors of children have typically confined acceptable poetry to acceptable topics: admiration, aspiration, just rewards, and realism. The beautiful and good are not the sole inhabitants of the world, and Silverstein is willing to admit to feeling angry, spiteful, depressed, prematurely world-weary, and unimpressed. He mentions the unmentionable, and absolutely no adults, except the sometimes credible persona of the poet as he seeks to advise and encourage, are admirable in this book. When they are present at all, which is infrequently, they are stupid and harmless enough to be ignored, or deranged.

The serious antiwar and racial-equality messages in this volume are clearly present but not dominant. These themes are not so obtrusive as to have gotten the book banned or placed on some list of censorable or controversial books—the bathroom humor is enough to do that. *Huck Finn* and Dr. Seuss's *Butter Battle Book* received more negative criticism for taking on these subjects. Neither of Silverstein's themes is presented in such a way that they are at all arguable; of course all people are equal under their skin; this is not a Caucasian versus African-American or Latino/Latina argument, not an argument about equal access to education or employment, but simply a basic affirmation of human goodness and value throughout the world. Wars such as the one fought by General Clay and General Gore, who are unable to articulate the reasons for their battling, are simply indefensible. The reference to the division that the Vietnam War caused our nation was clear to adults at the time that the book was written and is now but perhaps may not be to later generations of young readers. The Vietnam War was fought for no apparent reason; the question of the value of wars fought for high ideals, such as World War II, need not be addressed. And certainly, playing games of affection, such as Hug O' War, rather than more violent games and practicing acceptance rather than anger and revenge are unarguably good. War is Silverstein's one didactic issue, beyond encouraging human aspiration and imagination.

Sidewalk is a first-time effort in poetry for children by a writer who had considerable writing and illustrating experience. Silverstein was entering an arena of publishing dominated by teachers and librarians, who had rather strict guidelines for what was acceptable for children: serious, grand topics of beauty, expressed in elegant metrics and diction and suitable for developing morals and literary taste. Those young people for whom the book was written had mostly abandoned poetry as a subject suitable for school and homework but not much else. Silverstein's writing experience brought with it other experiences that challenged many of the assumptions, of both the teachers and librarians and of the children, about suitable topics and attitudes for poetry. On the whole, this volume signals a change in attitudes about children's poetry, in the messages in the poetry itself, the topics covered, the metrics, and the illustration.

There are enough joke poems in the book that the reader will turn the page, not simply set the book down. On the other hand, the understanding of a poem later in the book is not dependent on that of an earlier poem, so that the book can conveniently be set down and taken up again. Further, there are enough jokes in the book and enough poems about simple pleasures that the reader need not worry about relentless moralizing. The poetry is accessible, with no dense language and no hidden meanings, and communicates clearly with its intended audience, so clearly that the book shocked some adult readers who read the book after its first publication. While the poetic metrics are sometimes sloppy and inexact, especially in the rhymes, they lend an easy swing to the verse. The poems contain a variety of voices, none of which sounds like a teacher or preacher or parent.

The cartoon illustrations emphasize action and isolated detail rather than background and subtlety. The lack of a frame around each picture, as one would find on a cartoon panel in a periodical, gives the illustrations a sense of immediacy rather than of distance and objectivity. These are pictures to jump right into, not to contemplate and ponder; there are few important details or painterly effects, so even a quick read or view of the pictures makes their meanings clear. None of the illustrations is decorative, except those on the title, dedication, and index pages. All are integral to the experiences of the poems. The ample white space on the page and the typewriter typeface, whose letters are widely spaced, not kerned, give the page a sense of leisure and ease. Although poems are grouped, they are never crowded; on the other hand, the joining of two poems on a single two-page spread is not as successful visually or thematically. *A Light in the Attic* demonstrates Silverstein's ability to join two poems visually across a spread, their similarity of shape and theme more clearly bodied forth. The composition of *Sidewalk* suggests that each poem was conceived and illustrated separately, then arranged on the pages; *Attic* seems a more holistic effort.

Sidewalk was published at the same time as another landmark in popular literature for children, the volume *Free to Be . . . You and Me.*[13] This volume, a collection of stories, narratives, songs, and poems by various hands, had the avowed purpose of questioning stereotypes and of encouraging children to embrace life's possibilities rather than abide by limits. Sponsored by the Ms. Foundation, the book makes sexual stereotypes an obvious target. The human-potential movement comes to children in this book. In her foreword, Marlo Thomas, one of the book's guiding forces, claims that this is "a book of stories and poems and songs that would help boys and girls feel free to be who they are and who they want to be." She says that the book is deliberately unconventional: "Those of you who are looking for Wonderland or Prince Charming or a sleeping or even sleepy princess will not find them here. The world we care about here is the most adventurous, the largest, the most wondrous of all; the world of feeling and the land of ourselves" (*Free*, 9). Gloria Steinem talks about the "book's message of freedom" and the need to "get rid of old-fashioned systems based on sex and race" (p. 11). The afterword, by Kurt Vonnegut, is a bit less targeted, closer to Silverstein's feelings that children should not be offered simple answers to complex questions. As Vonnegut says, "A first grader should understand that his or her culture isn't a rational invention; that there are thousands of other cultures and they all work pretty well; that all cultures function on faith rather than truth; that there are lots of alternatives to our own society" (p. 139). Both Silverstein and Ursula Nordstrom contributed to this deliberately iconoclastic volume, which is similar to *Sidewalk* in that it is clearly informed by the emphasis on freedom from social restriction and respect for diversity.

Silverstein does not take on the issue of gender equality in his book, but he does talk about cultural assumptions and their actualization in inexplicable rules of etiquette. He celebrates and encourages the far reaches of the human imagination and the daring, and he articulates the less attractive and elsewhere unmentionable aspects of child life. Twenty years after its initial publication, this book is beginning to show its age; Jimmy Jet's TV set has no VCR, no cable access; the rabbit ears on top seem like antiques. The generals' warfare, which is hand to hand rather than technological or even nuclear, is equally antiquated, and the suggestion that love is all you need seems simpleminded given the world's continuing experiences of genocidal war. But bathrooms, butts, and siblings still continue to amuse and plague children, and admitting their existence and amusement, even in poetry, is unusual. This book continues to be read because Silverstein offers more accessible, realistic poetry to children than other poets have. It is found on the shelves in school libraries and classrooms, which indicates its acceptance as well as the continuing difficulties that Americans have in finding poetry that speaks to the popular ear.

Chapter Four
Poetry with the Electricity On

A Light in the Attic is far and away Shel Silverstein's best work for children, and the most daring. It was clearly designed as a book by itself and for itself rather than as a collection of pieces published elsewhere that were cut, pasted, tweaked, added to, and changed for book-length publication for youth readership, as was *Sidewalk*. The book's design speaks to Silverstein's focused effort and to his vision of the book as original work published for a single, intended market. From the cover to the final poem, the book has a clearer sense than does *Sidewalk* of its audience and the length of its narrative and better expresses children's interests, needs, and unspoken fears and desires. The acknowledgments page contains the only poem printed elsewhere and otherwise simply gives credit for inspirations from other people. The lack of acknowledgments again hints at the single-minded effort that Silverstein puts forth here. Ursula Nordstrom still receives her just mention, but there is no evidence of difficulties and coaxing between poet and editor, perhaps because Silverstein was more experienced and more sure of what he was doing in this volume.

There are fewer long poems here than in *Sidewalk*, none longer than a two-page spread, and thus none of *Sidewalk*'s text density. The shorter poems are grouped together across two-page spreads, each with its own illustration but usually with some unifying elements to the spread: a shared baseline horizon, a gesture on one page met by a responding gesture on another, or similar design elements from one illustration to the next. The simplicity of the illustration style in *Sidewalk* has been modified somewhat; Silverstein has produced more fine-line drawings and gives more detail to individual characters, but he still pays no great attention to background details. Background details are not Silverstein's strength, nor are they required in the cartoon style. Instead, he concentrates on individual caricature and action, and the characters' exaggerated features make their prominent characteristics all the more laughable.

In some ways, in spite of the lack of longer, more complex narrative poetry, *Attic* is a volume of poetry for a slightly older child than that intended for *Sidewalk*. There is more focus on school and schoolwork, more clever, artful dodging of adult prohibitions, and more wordplay. The several voices that Silverstein assumes as poet and adult are more coaxing and teasing, as if the child were more reticent and had more complex skills with which to avoid adults than the younger, more easily engaged child assumed in *Sidewalk*. On the other hand, there are fewer topical poems, none about war or race relations, the kinds of current events that Silverstein deals with in the earlier volume. Thus the target reader may not be any older or more mature. Perhaps Silverstein said all he had to about these subjects in *Sidewalk* and therefore chose, consciously or otherwise, to move on to new material here.

Organization

Like *Sidewalk*, *Attic*'s structure is typical of a volume of poetry in that it has an introductory poem and a concluding one. The book begins with the title poem, "A Light in the Attic," and repeats the cover illustration.[1] The illustration features a face with a forehead formed like the dormer of a house. The roof with a chimney peaks at the top of the head, and a window with open shutters reveals yet another small head, marked only by two eyes, peering out at the reader above the more complete facial features of the larger, expressionless face below. Someone is up in the attic peeking out the window, providing action, thought, and general brainpower to that lower face with the unfocused eyes. The poem is a variation on the old adage about the porch light being on but nobody being home; the light represents active intelligence.

The picture on the cover, which places the head on a background of stars, suggests a floating house or that the head is disembodied. Inside the book, however, the picture has no such celestial background and shows only the face, turned at a slight, off-center, critical angle. Thus the viewer focuses more tightly on the face and its emotionlessness without being distracted by the vast expanses of space in the background that the cover suggests. The poem itself is about the light in the attic being on and the speaker being able to see that light in spite of its hidden location behind shutters in a darkened house, or behind the blank stare of the head. The speaker lures the shy light out of hiding, gently teasing and coaxing. He or she then tries to make eye and voice contact to get the light to burn brightly and therefore get the intelligence and wit to play without reticence. The "flickerin' flutter" of the light suggests some kind of impediment to shining more brightly—is it shyness, or fear, or some other lack of will?

As Myra Cohn Livingston has said, Silverstein is trying to get the reader to turn on the light,[2] or, to use biblical language, to take the lamp from under the bushel and let it shine before the world. Although the biblical meaning might seem inappropriate for such a worldly poet as Silverstein, his discussions of God and God's actual presence later in the book support this reading of the poem, at least upon rereading the entire book. The shyness of the presumed audience is first sounded on the half-title page, where a childlike form peers out from behind an immense book; only the eyes and the hint of a nose are visible, a pose that indicates possessiveness about the book in the illustration as well as shyness about revealing self to the viewer. The imagery of light is picked up on the full-title page with a bare light bulb that hangs down next to the title, its switch clearly visible; the clear bulb on a white page makes it difficult to determine whether this light is on or off, but throughout the book, lights on and minds open is the preferred state of consciousness.

The cover's celestial theme is carried on throughout the book, from the second illustration, which shows someone swinging from a rope tied to a star far above a city below, to other poems about flying and about astronomical bodies, including God in his heaven above. The theme of the head and its various odd, detached, and changeable features also continues throughout the book. Sometimes these poems are quite odd, as in "Who Ordered the Broiled Face?" (112), in which the face is delivered on a platter. Sometimes Silverstein chooses to reflect on this theme, as in "Hinges" (135), which is about wishing heads were hinged so we could let all the "bad stuff" out and keep the good stuff in. The poems are, of course, appropriately illustrated with faces that have all sorts of odd parts. As the center of intelligence and identity, the head and face are clearly central to humanness and creativity. Silverstein's consistent reference to heads throughout the book shows not only his understanding of children and their jokes about heads but also his encouragement of weird as well as thoughtful uses for heads in general.

The final poem, which this time is not a series, as in *Sidewalk,* but stands alone, encourages the child to exert himself, both physically and imaginatively. "This Bridge" (168–69) recounts all of the book's adventures and glorious sights that the child has already experienced in the poet's company. The ending couplet sums up the poet's final stance about his efforts to amuse and the child's need to participate: "But this bridge will only take you halfway there— / The last few steps you'll have to take alone." In the last analysis, each person is dependent on individual effort and willingness to take risks. The final word "alone" suggests, quite accurately, that there are some things, including poetry, amusement, and imagination, that are the ultimate responsibility only of the individual. Poets can provide passing pleasure, as can illustrators. But to continue on a path of lively life experience, child readers must take responsibility for their own mental actions and activities. If the light is on in the attic, if the child reader makes use of active intelligence, then making progress over the second half of the bridge to even more fun and adventure will not be difficult.

The precariousness of being only halfway there, even at the end of the book, is dramatically portrayed in a single illustration that fully fills the two-page spread. The bridge of the poem's title starts on the lower left side of the left page, its arch continuing upward and across to the right page, following the path that the reader or viewer typically follows in reading, or surveying, an illustration. Unfortunately, this is only a half-bridge; the small, barely defined character looks out on its promontory to the space below; the bridge must be finished to meet the other side, where the exotic onion-topped towers and crenelated forts and pyramids lie. Without some kind of plan to build, some leap, or some imaginary construct that will permit return to the ground below, the character will be frozen in space, unable to return or go forward.

Luckily, the place from which to leap seems quite clear; the unfinished bridge resembles a diving board, already bent and ready to toss the child up and over to the other side. But without effort and perhaps some daring on their part, children will be stuck halfway, neither here nor there. Here Silverstein is urging children to take an active role in their futures; they should not permit life just to happen but take some action—almost any action—to shape it. Standing still, settling only for the experience of the book and going no further, is simply not an option. The poem's serious tone works as a counterbalancing conclusion for all the silliness the rest of the book contains; Silverstein is not without didactic purpose in this volume, and he sends the child reader forth to try out some of the lessons he has taught. As the book's closing poem, "This Bridge" functions as a summation of Silverstein's attitude toward childhood and maturity. Ultimately, each individual is alone, with only the encouragement of others to rely on. But each individual carries responsibility for his or her own success. Fortunately, most everyone has the ability to turn on the light in the attic, and with some risk-taking, most everyone can succeed, even gloriously. There is no sense of being left hanging here, with no place to go, as at the end of *Sidewalk*'s "Search." One step, one leap forward, and the reader is moving on. This is a much more satisfying ending than in the earlier volume. The forward motion is already behind the reader, who has only to follow through. *Attic*'s organization seems both easier and yet tighter than that of *Sidewalk*. On the one hand, Silverstein seems to be working less hard at being poetic; the serious poems take on serious topics but succeed better. The organization across a page turn is easier to see, both because the two-page spread is used more effectively to illustrate two poems at the same time and because the poems seem to be grouped in more obvious ways. The reader does not need to ponder the connection between the two poems facing each other because either the illustration or the topics make the connection clear. Some poems are so metrically easy that they are not really poems at all but dialogues set in short lines, like a joke or a story in prose set to look like poetry. The wordplays come easily, and the diction is common, not occasionally elevated and archaic, as it sometimes is in *Sidewalk*. Overall, Silverstein is trying less hard to be poetic and succeeding better in illustrating what he does produce, whether or not it is technically poetry.

Themes and Topics

Attic is Silverstein's most daring book because it picks up those themes of physical exposure in his *Playboy* cartooning that are appropriate for children, if offensive to adults. There are many bare butts in this book, including one that has been stung by a "Spelling Bee" (81), which spells out "Hello . . . You've been stung by a bee" across the exposed lower cheeks. A forgetful character in "Something Missing" (26) remembers to put on everything except his pants when he gets dressed. Of course, his absent-mindedness is fully illustrated. The most disgusting poem, "Quick Trip" (116–19), a four-line poem that stretches across four pages, is about the "quick-digesting Gink," a monster who eats children, passes them through his digestive tract, and excretes them unharmed on the final page, where they tumble out without a mark on them. Without using a single word about feces and without showing the actual act of elimination, the poem implies the unmentionable without actually breaching propriety. Although this poem does not actually deal with exposure, it does speak about the unspeakable and is more raunchy than the poems found in *Sidewalk*. And yet the four-line poem does not say directly what it so obviously means, and so Silverstein avoids getting into difficulty with censors.

Attic is also the only book in which Silverstein approaches issues of sex and sexiness. The cumulative effect of this book, which is filled with deflated hopes, jokes at the expense of others, poems about arguing, and the unnatural strictures that parents place on children, is like that of an emotional roller coaster; it is a tour de force of crazy people and crazy ideas. A last attempt at daring to offend and breach conventions about appropriate topics for children, "They've Put a Brassiere on the Camel" (166–67) is funny at least partly because of the camel's exposure and its wearing of unmentionable lingerie. But it is also funny because of the way the brassiere is shown fitting the camel: across the two humps. No other animal would be quite so appropriate; the camel's full gaze, slightly lopsided, with heavy-lidded chagrin, is focused on the reader. This frank eye contact of illustration with viewer is usually limited to characters who wish to be admired by the reader, as Nodelman notes;[3] here the admiration turns to guffaw because of the brassiere's silly fit and the unnecessary covering of an animal that is difficult to make sexy at all. The eye contact admits the reader/viewer into the inner circle of those who understand how ridiculous this attempt at decency is—and children are part of this circle.

The people who perpetrate this odd act are referred to simply as "they," the same "they" of common parlance who typify stupidity and rigidity; among children, "they" are also usually adults, and by referring to authorities as "they," Silverstein effectively distances himself from their camp and their stupidity. "They" force the camel into the underwear to make it "decent" and "respectable," even though a quick glance at the picture shows how dramatically they have failed. There is nothing indecent about the camel in the first place, and the act simply draws attention to the animal rather than making it more acceptable and less noticeably flagrant in some violation of propriety. The poem is really about nudity, and laughing at it for its inherent appeal to children, rather than about sex issues. This animal has no sex appeal and would offend no one; the camel wearing the brassiere is more shocking than the animal in its natural state.

In this book, Silverstein celebrates nudity for its naturalness and pleasure and displays it not because it is funny but because it feels good. In the vein of feeling natural and being in touch with one's own pleasures and feelings, Silverstein offers "Tryin' On Clothes" (76). The young speaker tries on a farmer's hat and a dancer's shoes, finding neither comfortable or useful. Finally, the child tries on "the summer sun" and "the grass beneath bare feet" and finds both pleasurable, concluding that "[n]ature's clothes just fit me best." The poem admits the full-body experience of clothes as well as fresh air. It's not as much a matter of how clothes look but more about how they feel from the inside. The speaker in this poem insists that they be comfortable. The humorous theme of exposure here surfaces slyly in the last stanza; until this point, clothes shopping is limited to hats and shoes. Being natural and true to one's self and not trying to fit in someone else's shoes—or hat—sometimes means being unconventional. Being one with nature and one's natural self does not always mean disrobing, but a wholeness of self is certainly one of the messages here. Even the exposure joke is a small one; this is a poem not of high hilarity but rather of quiet satisfaction and all-encompassing comfort. The illustration does not offer a public display of nudity but rather impishly reveals a small person, whose upper torso is half hidden by the farmer's enormous, floppy hat, trying on the shoes. The face is not visible, and the rump appears clothed by shorts of some kind. There is no embarrassed look at the viewer, no gaze seeking to engage at all but simply the act of trying on clothes in dress-up play, as Silverstein describes in the early part of the poem. Although there is plenty of rear-end nudity in this book, Silverstein manages to move the issue on from humor to more weighty issues of naturalness.

Serious Issues

Attic does not degenerate into a series of silly jokes about bathroom subjects and others that dare to be inappropriate. There are the odd characters and short poems of one-line jokes, but Silverstein also takes up serious issues, well spaced between jokes that are nonetheless weighty and important. Silverstein adopts a tone of serious social concern only once, in one of the most memorable poems, "The Little Boy and the Old Man" (95). The meeting of the minds of both young and old is simply yet poignantly and movingly depicted. The boy opens by describing the pain he feels in his treatment by adults, who should know better than to be so thoughtless. His embarrassed admissions, about being unable to control his bladder, about being unable to control eating utensils, about crying, about being ignored, all meet with sympathetic admission by the old man of similar treatment and circumstances. In the boy's final complaint, that "[g]rown-ups don't pay attention to me," he is engaged both physically and empathetically with the old man: the "warmth of a wrinkled old hand" is reassuring and comforting, especially because the old man admits that he is ignored by adults too.

The circularity of youth and old age is almost Shakespearean, recalling the nine ages of man in which the last stage of life, old age, mimics the first stage, infancy. In this poem, however, the similarity between the two stages is based on mistreatment rather than on physical inability. The poem is devastating in its treatment of adults, those in control who might admit that at least old people are fully human if they cannot admit the same of children. But the shame they inflict and their utter disregard indict the middle-aged from both ends of the age spectrum. The old man reassures the child that embarrassing lapses are not so embarrassing and laughs as he acknowledges his own shortcomings. But such laughter is not possible at the end—abuse and neglect cannot be shrugged off so easily.

But as is typical throughout this book, Silverstein does not remain on this ponderous, sad note, nor does he repeat it. Instead, the poem is placed quite appropriately between one about babies and one about indulgent grandparents. "Rockabye" (95), which precedes and faces "Little Boy," provides a lead-in with its sympathetic treatment of babies. The poem deals with the baby in the lullabye who is swinging in the treetop. The speaker duly points out the precariousness of the perch and indirectly acknowledges the sibling rivalry the lullabye inspires in the last two lines: "Baby, I think someone down here's / Got it in for you." The baby looks out from the basket, only its wide, surprised, perhaps fearful eyes visible on an otherwise bald, featureless head. The basket, woven of rope, seems more like an imprisoning net than a cradle.

Most explicators of "Rock-a-bye Baby" point out the contradiction between its rather violent words and the quiet, comfortable melody that accompanies them. It is not hard to reach the conclusion that the sentiments express an older sibling's disdain for the arrival of a baby in the family. In Silverstein's poem, the speaker stands on the ground with the person who is the source of the vengefulness; in fact, it is possible that they are one and the same person. The poem points obliquely at a sibling as the perpetrator of jealousy but in a voice that seeks to caution in a helpful way. Although it is probably not Silverstein's intention to help explicate the original lullabye, his poem does again raise the question that the original does: why are the baby and cradle up in the tree in the first place? Who would place a baby at risk, and why is this an appropriate occasion for a lullabye at all?

This poem's placement, preceding "The Little Boy and the Old Man" on the left side of the two-page spread, suggests a balance between the topics, of babies and old people, and suggests a topical connection between the two poems. The placement of "The Little Boy and the Old Man" makes sense in terms of the coupling of poems in each spread and of the reader's expectation of such a connection by page 95. That "The

Little Boy and the Old Man" is not illustrated is also not surprising. The relationship between the two characters, which would have to be established in an illustration, is not so important. Rather, it is the commonality of past experience and opposition to grown-ups that unites them. "The Little Boy and the Old Man" is not a poem about action or silly caricature, so Silverstein's typical cartoon technique would not be particularly effective in extending the poem's meaning. Without illustration, the poem deals even more centrally with language and feeling. There are other poems in the book that are not illustrated, to the similar good effect of focusing on language and theme.

What is unexpected is that "The Little Boy and the Old Man" is followed by "Surprise" (96–97) after the page turn. "Surprise" is a poem about an entirely different kind of old man, an indulgent, world-traveling grandfather. This old man is not oppressed by the world but is a master of it in his travels. He sends wonderful gifts through the mail to his grandchildren from all the exotic places he visits. It would appear that the grandfather's ports of call are chosen by the poet not just for their wide span across the globe but also for the possibilities their names offer for rhyming. For example, a "cockatoo" arrives from "Katmandu"; "Myrtle Beach" rhymes with "a turtle each"; and "an iguana came" rhymes with "from Spain." Now grandfather is "in India," which narrows the possibilities of what might be in the oddly shaped box in the illustration. One of the grandchildren looks up at its sizable bulk with eager anticipation. The other, who is smaller, turns away fearfully, echoing the baby's appearance in "Rockabye," with only eyes and hairless head to define his face.

The poem's text is on the left-hand side of the spread, above and to the left of the illustration, which the reader is likely to consider both before and after reading the poem. The large box stands on four legs, with eyeholes and a trunk outlined by nailed boards. In spite of its boarded and obscuring surface, the box obviously contains an elephant, which connects with the poem's title: the surprise is an elephant. The final line, "My Grandpa always thinks of me," can be seen as a child's unequivocal assessment of the gifts, especially since grandparents are seldom so exotic or extravagant as to send wild animals. The desire to have a circus of odd animals is one most children understand, and the arrival of an elephant is a wish come true.

On the other hand, a slightly older child reader will see the fear in the younger child's eyes and begin to question the gift's appropriateness. The "smelly goat" from Spain is not exactly described as an ideal pet from a truly thoughtful grandparent, and the elephant may be just as problematic. If it's the thought that counts, not the gift, one can justly wonder what this giver had in mind. Could it be revenge on the children's parents? In light of the previous poem about the nastiness of the middle-aged, this is a possibility. In any case, the odd packaging and the unlikelihood of an elephant arriving through normal shipping channels makes the poem so fantastic that the more serious considerations about grandparents and their understanding of gifts are unlikely. As an antidote to the earlier poem about the sadness of childhood and old age, this poem succeeds in reestablishing grandparents as active, exotic sources of enjoyment. Silverstein's ability to consider the circumstances of people of all ages signals a mature viewpoint here. The wide range of ages suggests that simple dichotomies in perspective are just a start in considering the range of possibilities in life.

The other poem of particularly evocative power in this volume is "Whatif" (90). The contraction of the question "what if" to a single, rapidly spoken word signals the conversational tone here, which mimics oral speech, and the torment of the whatifs as they are fired off obsessionally by the child speaker. The ability to consider the possibilities of life, to ask the question "what if," marks the reader's level of maturity as well. "What ifs" are possibilities that normal children's questioning, probing minds can entertain only if they have enough life experience to look beyond the present moment and situation and see that there are other possibilities beyond. Here, the "whatifs" are all negative, the kinds of large and small torments that worry children but that adults frequently have enough experience to set aside as unlikely or unimportant or in some way remediable. The poem does a remarkable job of describing the thought processes of the insomniac and the kinds of anxieties that keep children awake at night. Some of the child narrator's questions are trivial; "What if the bus is late?" has an easy answer: there's not much you can do about it, so why worry?

But Silverstein's narrator does not balk at confronting some of life's most unthinkable possibilities: "What if I get sick and die? / . . . What if my parents get divorced?" Silverstein balances the horrifying, the trivial, and the fantastic in the list of "whatifs" by alternating them throughout the poem. His child narrator does not hesitate to bring the topics up, indicating here a new level of boldness and authenticity of the child's experience. Children do think these thoughts, in the rapid-fire, depressing quantity in which Silverstein presents them and in nighttime isolation from comfort. Admitting that such possibilities exist, in writing, in a volume of poetry, does nothing to reassure the child except to give voice to ideas that otherwise go unspoken in the middle of the night. Simply admitting that other people, even children, think like this puts Silverstein and this volume on the leading edge of describing childhood experience honestly and fully. If part of the poet's obligation is to tell the truth, Silverstein takes on this responsibility fully and authentically, especially in this poem.

In "Deaf Donald" (143), Silverstein deals with the serious issue of physical disability. Donald signs "I love you" in a rebus illustration to Talkie Sue. Unfortunately, he cannot communicate with her. She is unable to "listen" to his sign language, and so his love goes unrequited. Perhaps the failing here is hers, though she is not really the poem's focus, as its title suggests. That she does not know how to listen in his language is thoughtless, but it is Donald's loss and society's lack of understanding of the deaf that get serious attention in this poem. This poem is part of the tradition of unrequited love and mismatches among unequals seen in *Sidewalk* and occasionally elsewhere in *Attic;* the theme of "The Oak and the Rose" (165), in which the oak simply grows out of reach of the smaller rose, is closer to that of the personal-freedom poems discussed later. But the focus in "Deaf Donald" on a missed opportunity for love between an appropriately lovable man and a thoughtless woman make this poem less humorous and more poignant, especially because it deals with a lack of understanding about disabilities.

Of course, this poem provides no solutions to mainstream society's ignorance of the disabled. It is another interlude between the humorous poems and those with more serious intent. But even the humorous poems have trenchant points. For example, the difficulty of answering questions, especially those posed in simpleminded dichotomies, is also a theme in this book. In "Zebra Question" (125), a child speaker asks the animal, "Are you black with white stripes? / Or white with black stripes?" The zebra, normally considered a gentle animal, prey, not predator, acts out of character. It retorts with a barrage of personal questions to the speaker about being mostly good or bad, being noisy, happy, neat, or their opposites. The questions are posed with an edge, but they point to the fact that people—and animals—cannot be adequately defined by simple either/or oppositions. The child speaker is duly chastised and silenced at poem's end, and the zebra's rapid, colloquial piling up of questions certainly puts the child speaker off. The child reader, on the other hand, rather than being silenced into submission, is likely to challenge logical assumptions about the world, to go beyond either/or

and realize that there are gradations between opposites, other possibilities than simply the most obvious or its reverse. The nature of opposites,
the immaturity of oppositional thinking, and the logical tools of analysis
are raised in such poems as this. These themes force the child reader
beyond the easy, simple assumptions and solutions that children so easily embrace in their early stages of socialization and that adults sometimes offer in situations that children realize are much more complicated. In this way, *Attic* is much more aggressive than *Sidewalk* in
challenging children's thinking patterns and in helping them experience
more than the volume's humor. Life is more complicated than either a
simple answer or a funny joke.

"Zebra" faces another poem that is an extended pun that goes
beyond simple wordplay. "Nobody" (124) starts out with the cheap theatrics of the disappointed child: "Nobody loves me, / Nobody cares."
The speaker has nobody for a friend, nobody for an admirer, but then
looks around for a personified Nobody and finds, instead, somebody.
This particular pun is as old as Homer's Cyclops in the *Odyssey* but certainly has an up-to-date appearance here. Suddenly the lament about
nobody is banished, and "Nobody's gone!" This inability to remain
morose is characteristic of youth and its easily changeable moods that
make clinical depression unlikely. But the poem's pun, that nobody is
actually a person, prepares the way for the "Zebra Question" on the following page. The puns, the stupid questions, the simplistic thinking
gone awry are all sources of humor as well as pointers to the book's
deeper questions and considerations. The longer the poem, the more
likely it is that Silverstein is getting at something more than a punch
line or a joke.

Further exploring the themes of opposites, Silverstein shows that
simple opposition can depend on angle or perspective in the poem
"Backward Bill" (40–41). Bill is a cowboy who pursues backwardness
obsessively, like a limerick character, but who is given great range to display the various ways in which things can oppose one another. He pays
his boss on payday, describes his wife as "[m]y own true hate," and even
reverses letters in onomatopoeias. For example, his gun goes "GNAB,"
though it is still a gun, not a nug; his spurs "neigh" and his horse goes
"clang." Reversal is applied in a variety of ways here, and Bill remains
happy, never reversing his disposition, as he rides off, not backs off, into
the sunset, not the sunrise, "a-carryin' his hoss" at the end of the poem.
On the right page, facing his poem to the left, Bill rides off with a broad
smile, his horse facing anxiously and antiprogressively to the left while

Bill faces right, an apt illustrational representation of his life circumstance: which way is he going? Reversal depends on how it is pursued and how relentlessly, but in any case it is a source of humor as well as a thought pattern with which to investigate serious issues. Silverstein shows his willingness to take on any subject and any authority in the poetry in *Attic* about God. "Importnt?" (*sic*, 54) begins with deep consideration by suggesting that an individual's most appropriate stance is humility before God. In the poem, an extended discussion between two letters of the alphabet, lowercase *a* and capital *G*, the *a* asserts its central place in many words and therefore in the existence of the things those words describe—such as heaven and earth. After this boastful speech, capital *G* shows graphically that this proud assumption is not true—the words are still understandable even when the *a* is missing. As *G* says, "Nd erth nd heven still would be, / Without thee." Even with the missing vowel, this line is readable. Silverstein's use of the archaic "thee" signals a different kind of diction and topic than his usual colloquial, informal tone and subject. Although the voice of big *G* sounds normal and humanly reasonable, the language of prayer and of religious discourse appears at the end in the final word. No one but God should assume such importance as little *a* has mistakenly taken on. The two letters are shown conversing with each other on something soft, like a cloud—perhaps this conversation is happening in heaven; the *a* is shaped like a typeface "a", and his head seems bowed in humility over his belly. The large *G* seems to talk down to him, but not in his stance or tone of reprimand: he simply looks down from on high. The poem's humor, which is quite mild, is all at the expense of the braggart little *a*. Is this Silverstein's indirect way of calling the little *a* a little ass?

Elsewhere, Silverstein is more irreverent about God, but gently so and with a firm layer of humor. "God's Wheel" (152) offers a child the possibility of taking on God's job of steering the world. The child then starts bargaining, like a job applicant in an interview or a selfish child taking on chores: "How much do I get?" is the most crass request of several that question God's job in task-specific terms. The child does not see this as a great opportunity but as just another chore, and he sees God as an employer or parent capable of being manipulated. God's conclusion is the right one: "I don't think you're quite ready yet." The child has an argumentative tone, and the way he thinks about the job and his understanding of the nature of its responsibility are sadly immature. The poem is a humorous one; not many children or poets or even prophets or apostles get to argue so successfully with God.

Although "God's Wheel" poses no deep or difficult questions, the idea of talking to God in tones other than prayerful ones breaks new ground in poetry for children. In the illustration, a child figure behind a steering wheel directs the world. Even Silverstein does not attempt to illustrate God directly, leaving the task instead to such greater artistic talents as Michelangelo. Silverstein does take on the nature of human evil in "Hinges" (135), which suggests that evil could be removed from human brains in a kind of lobotomy if only the skull gave convenient access through the "hinges" mentioned in the title. But this is a short poem and does not demand or require much contemplation. The divine presence, which appears in this book intermittently, is usually ready to contribute to a heavenly joke.

Housework, Homework, Otherwork

Other such poems of authenticity appear in the volume, though they are not as devastating; instead, the poet finds a lighter, more humorous vein. "The Homework Machine" (56) describes a child using what most children want. Few homework exercises are designed to engage a child enough to make them attractive. With the considerable range of machines available to take the drudgery out of so much of what goes on in the house, and the inventor's idealization and cleverness, it is not surprising that so many children have wanted a homework machine and have fantasized about building one. The contraption shown here is full of Rube Goldberg reels and conveyor belts and gears and is, as the narrator says, the "most perfect contraption that's ever been seen." The vocative "oh" in the first line, in which the narrator sings the praises of this wonderful invention, suggests the speaker's lyrical, expansive state of mind at the poem's opening.

The first homework question that the speaker asks of the machine is one of simple addition: "nine plus four?," to which the perfect machine incorrectly responds, "[T]hree." The speaker's distress is deflating and understated, especially in comparison to the joyous extravagance of the opening: "Oh me . . ." This is clearly not a functional appliance, as any child might have predicted. It is not even as good as a common calculator. Although the poem stands on its own for reading and recitation, the picture of the magnificent machine further manifests Silverstein's intention by adding an explanation to the machine's shortcomings: inside, a small, babylike child is doing the actual work, scribbling answers on pieces of paper. Like many of children's homemade machines, it is more for show than for real effectiveness. This is one of Silverstein's machines that does not seem dated; even though the illustration shows a contraption that uses a tape like that of an adding machine, it still looks complicated enough to impress even children of the electronic, digital age.

One of the book's most effective themes is Silverstein's conspiracy with his child readers to avoid work and get what they want out of their parents, a continuation of the theme sounded in "The Homework Machine." The shorter poem "How Not to Have to Dry the Dishes" (12) suggests that children should drop a dish in order to avoid being asked to help out with that chore again. With knowing slyness that children will recognize, Silverstein rightly assesses this tactic's likelihood of success. His objection to doing that job is that it is "[s]uch an awful, boring chore," not that it is difficult. He does not suggest that all chores are boring, but compared to running errands, the alternative suggested in the poem, dish drying pales, though it is a typical assignment for children. Even those who live with kitchens appointed with the convenience of a dishwasher find themselves having to unload the dishes and put them away, part of the duty that the chore of drying usually entails. The repetition of the line "If you have to dry the dishes" echoes adult insistence that children comply, no matter what oral or physical resistance they may offer.

The fact that dropping a dish may result in being forbidden to dry the dishes turns the tables on adults, who in this poem are ominously referred to as "they," the unidentified oppressors of childhood. Like the "they" in Edward Lear's limericks, "they" in this poem are traditional child-rearers who demand children's assistance in household tasks, especially those that are boring. For modern children, whose labor in such tasks as tending flocks or carrying wood is not required for the household's economic operation, mundane chores are more common. As a uniformly nondescript mass, "they" deserve all the objections and manipulations they get from children, who "they" seem to assume need to be oppressed in order to grow up right.

The slyness of the solution here mirrors the cleverness children develop during their school years in manipulating their parents and conniving their way out of work. The accompanying illustration of a little girl drying a dish nearly half her size indicates just how onerous and unmanageable the task is. Her hiding behind the dish, glancing furtively out at the reader from behind the huge circle of porcelain, accurately reflects the speaker's collusion with the listener and viewer. At the girl's foot is a broken dish; her eyes appear to glance out at the reader and down to the plate in simultaneous glee and anxiety. Perhaps the effect will not be what she wishes and she'll be reprimanded rather than forbidden to dry the dishes again. Perhaps her furtiveness is shame. The "maybe" in the line "Maybe they won't let you dry the dishes anymore" clues readers in to the possibility that taking such a course of action just might not work. On the other hand, the poem's humor and tactic go a long way toward convincing a child of the possibility that events may just fall out the way that Silverstein suggests.

Avoiding work at all is a consistent theme throughout *Attic*. "Tired" (78) is the complaint of someone who has worked hard all day, watching nature pass by while performing such energy-consuming tasks as "holding the grass in its place" and "[t]iming the sun to see what time it sets." This speaker even finds it draining to take "twelve thousand and forty-one breaths." The litany of activities certainly describes a passive day but one of some interest, as it shows a mind actively at work even while the body is physically at rest. This is not a bored, idle mind but an active, cataloging one. The repeated claim that "I'm tired!," which is given extra emphasis by the full capitalization of "TIRED!" in the final line, seems incredible at first glance. But at second consideration the poem's action gives children a model to follow in finding subjects of interest and focus. The poem accurately describes how children sometimes fill up their time, having little to show for it but having expended much energy nonetheless. Sometimes just growing and playing takes energy, just as more laborious kinds of work do. The work here is not measured by outcomes and productivity but by interest and noteworthiness. It is difficult to imagine that all children reading this poem would find it humorous. The experienced and world weary might find it laughable, and certainly the lengthy catalog of useless tasks would add to that effect. Those used to chores would see the joke. On the other hand, children who are less knowledgeable and more open to the interests of these quite ordinary experiences, those who are more easily able to invest themselves in these activities, might find the poem accurate and straightforward, realistic in its assertion of weariness at the end of the day. Growing up and carefully observing the world really are hard work.

Avoiding work or any other obligation as defined by or insisted on by adults is one of this volume's sly, consistent messages. Exactly what "Hurk" (50) is is not clear to the speaker or to the reader, but whatever it is, it is certainly preferable to "work," its rhyme word. Playing tennis is quite obviously preferable to going to the "dentist," with which it rhymes; "soccer" rhymes with a visit to the "doctor" and has obviously superior interest. "Work," however, is so unspeakably objectionable that Silverstein need not elaborate on the attractions of hurk. Nowhere does he proclaim the dignity and fulfillment of work or chores, the most common form of work for children. He seems to acknowledge that a chore is unpleasant simply because it is an obligation. The perversity of human nature, to feel that an activity is onerous when required, but pleasurable when it is optional, is a quirk that Silverstein explores here, as Mark Twain did with Tom Sawyer's whitewashing the picket fence. The acknowledgment of this quirk, by an adult who clearly sympathizes with children, again resonates with authenticity to children's experience.

Boredom

The flip side of avoiding work is finding something to occupy oneself, especially one's mind. Although a resourceful child will find the tasks described in "Tired" highly entertaining, most children have not been taught the ways of creativity and useful leisure. Children of the television age have found the entertainment therein so accessible and easy that they have difficulty finding other sources of entertainment or mental absorption. Nor do children have purposeful work to do to be helpful and useful to the family and household. Constantly thrust into the position of consumers, children have not found ways to amuse themselves or occupy their time but simply consume the benefits of their care without needing to return the effort. The thrills offered on television and in other electronic forms of entertainment leave them looking for more. Without their electronic equipment, children frequently do not know what to do. Boredom, or waiting for engagement, is a common emotion for the modern child, one that adults may not understand since it is a new condition in child life. Certainly adults are not always sympathetic to boredom.

Silverstein acknowledges the prevalence of boredom here in several poems. "Channels" (87) describes television's inability to satisfy, as the child flicks the dial, proceeding numerically through channels that are sometimes nonfunctional, at other times full of "jive." The changes in television technology date this poem; the pace of the channel-changing here does not mimic rapid channel-surfing by remote control but rather the more deliberate, slightly slower flicking and crunching of a dial. Even in older technology, channel one was fictional and is present here mostly for the opportunity to rhyme "one" with "no fun," signaling the poem's attitude toward channels throughout. The reason to stop at channel 10 in the list of deficient entertainment values is partly because 10 short-comings are more than enough to convince the reader of television's inadequacies. But the list also stops at 10 because there were few channels beyond that in the television era before cable and public television.

In any case, the concluding question to the reader, "Wouldn't you like to *talk* awhile?," is a sensible alternative and one that indicates an interest in human interaction rather than electronic passivity. The offer of conversation is one seldom made to children, and its art is being lost. But talking to others is an alternative to the boredom that sometimes overwhelms children in their abilities to find other sources of entertainment. "Channels" is unillustrated, graphically reflecting the channels' emptiness and the lack of visual interest that even an illustrator as creative as Silverstein can bring to boredom. The illustration from the previous page intrudes slightly at the bottom. But the large white space of the page surrounding the essentially vertical poem emphasizes the brevity of the list of the various channels' inadequacies and is an appropriate illustrational reflection of the boredom that television can offer.

Elsewhere, Silverstein is even more dramatic in his portrayal of boredom. "Bored" (110) and "Standing Is Stupid" (111) face each other across a two-page spread. A simple illustration of a boy with a long board spans the two poems. In comparison to the more detailed illustrations elsewhere, this two-page spread is sparse, though the illustration contributes a visual pun. The title of the first poem is a pun on the word "board"; adding the prefixes "skate-", "out-", and "surf-" to "board" makes for more interesting words than "board" alone, but the single piece of lumber is all that the speaker can afford. Although he is clearly able to imagine other possibilities for his board and provides the reader with some linguistic humor in the playfulness of his language, the reader can understand why he is "bored." Only the title suggests the speaker's mental state, but his inability to use the plain board in active, interesting, adventuresome ways is enough to make the title convincing. The boy's nearly blank, somewhat quizzical expression and his static pose with his board starkly reflect his inner state. Although cartooning usually emphasizes action, this particular cartoon boy is as static as his board.

The poem on the right page, "Standing Is Stupid" (111), more fully develops the theme of boredom; clearly the illustration that spans the two pages belongs to the poem on the left-hand page, though the feeling of boredom is more accurately described in the poem on the right. Absolutely every activity the speaker can think of is useless. The activities' emptiness is underscored by the alliteration in many of the lines. "Sitting is senseless" is the most soundful, though the unusual diction in "[h]opping is hopeless" is equally devastating. The speaker's conclusion, "I'll go upstairs and / Lie down again," seems a fitting ending to all the useless activities he has described. The board/bored pun still resonates at the end of "Standing Is Stupid," especially because the end of the board, which has a nail in it, is visible at the end of the poem like a final punctuation point. Will the speaker be stiff as a board when he lies down? Will he lie down on the nail? Now, there is a possibility that offers some excitement and humor. Fortunately, a two-page spread, even with the illustration's unspoken humor finishing it off, is as long as Silverstein pursues the subject of boredom; enough is enough.

Poetry as Freedom

Fortunately for the bored, postmodern child, Silverstein offers alternatives to boredom even while acknowledging its enervating effects and its overwhelming presence in children's lives. One possibility is the passive but highly engaging activities listed in "Tired" (78), discussed earlier. Others include writing poetry or simply being silly, which Silverstein encourages early on in the book in the poem "Put Something In" (22). Such creative acts as drawing, writing "a nutty poem," singing, and dancing, no matter what the quality of the performance, are all encouraged by the poem's speaker, who at the end summarizes what all these activities can do: "Put something silly in the world / That ain't been there before." The slang word "ain't" strikes a note of informality about such performances and encourages children to be silly, easy, and outrageous in their efforts. Being silly is something that children frequently outgrow as they are civilized into adulthood. But Silverstein's message here is that one can be a contributing member of society simply by contributing something silly. Although the work ethic that has dominated this country has suggested that adulthood is a time of productive seriousness, Silverstein stands as a model of an adult who has made something silly and who clearly has given pleasure to children and many adults. The volume stands as an artifact, a witness to the value of silliness and the pleasure that it gives. Silverstein's encouragement of such behavior among children gains approval by his own efforts as well as by the pleasure he seems to assure children they will get and give in such activity.

The freedom to pursue activities and destiny to whatever far ends they lead, the necessity of remaining true to oneself and to nature, and the encouragement to pursue the unconventional are themes from the era in which *Attic* was written that Silverstein explores throughout. To value freedom and self-actualization was so common in the 1970s that it became a cliché in the 1980s, but the permission to defy societal strictures was a new idea and continues to be of value to children, who sometimes need encouragement to be creative risk takers. The book's hippie nudity is as much a legacy of Silverstein's reflecting on the freedom movement as it is a remnant of his *Playboy* cartooning or an apt understanding of the humor children find in exposure. In exploring individual freedom, Silverstein is picking up the theme sounded in "Tree House," from *Sidewalk;* here he takes the theme even further.

The ultimate ends of such individual freedom are suggested in "Eight Balloons" (58), all of which take off from their bunch to pursue adventures, such as contact with cacti, porcupines, and frying bacon. The saddest of the lot is the one that "sat around 'til his air ran out—WHOOSH!" All the rest end with a "POP!," which is what Silverstein commends in the final couplet: "Free to float and free to fly / And free to pop where they wanted to." All the balloons, even the one that sits still, are involved in activities of their own choice. They are not bound together as a group by some unthinking herd mentality, all eight committed to the same activity without other options. Each chooses its own adventure and by that choice its own end, and all eight end with a loud noise, gloriously rather than ignobly. Certainly their ends are more interesting than simply sitting around waiting to be bought, or being ignored. The repetition of the word "free" and the pleasures connoted by the words "float" and "fly," the alliterative quality of all three together, and the illustration all counteract the possibility that the balloons' ends are tragic. The illustration, which depicts all eight balloons floating above the text like party decorations, makes it difficult to see the poem as a whole in a tragic light. First and foremost, this is a celebration of happy endings, a variation on Silverstein's more usual use of the punch line—there is no reversal here but simply a different understanding of what coming to one's end might mean.

"Ations" (59) faces "Eight Balloons" on the right-hand page, the second half of what appears to be a party invitation, one of the few remaining formalities in children's lives in the late twentieth century. The illustration, which appears below the text, is of a small couple, a boy and a girl, bowing and curtseying one to the other in a deep formal bend. In fact, it is the formalities of human interaction and their labels that concern the poem. Each couplet ends in a word with the suffix *-ation*, the

Latinate ending that makes verbs into more stable nouns. There is a sensible progression to these words: "salutation," "communication," "altercation," "reconciliation," for example. The poem's purpose is clear in the penultimate couplet: "And all these ations added up / Make civilization." The poem is a tour de force of precise rhyming, which contradicts Silverstein's less rigorous approach to poetic technique elsewhere; therein lies part of the humor. For Silverstein, civilization is no more than fancy words and manners. Perhaps it's not really as big a deal as adults claim, and certainly the light touch at the end pokes fun of civilized behavior. The final couplet ends with a parenthetical remark by the poet: "(And if I say this is a wonderful poem, / Is that exaggeration?)." Perhaps it is, but this is one of Silverstein's more witty and exact efforts. As a counterpoint to "Eight Balloons," this poem suggests that freedom from the manners and language of civilization would be a whole lot more interesting and satisfying. Exaggerated manners are for parties and are not worth much elsewhere.

"Adventures of a Frisbee" (70) continues the theme of exploring possibilities while being true to oneself and one's own basic nature. The poem details the life of a Frisbee who

> got tired of sailing
> To and fro and to;
> And thought about the other things
> That he might like to do.

Accordingly, on his next toss, he takes off to explore the world, trying on various roles that suit his shape: eyeglasses, dinner plate, pizza, hubcap, phonograph record, quarter. Finding that none of these roles exactly fits his shape, desires, or other characteristics, he returns summarily to his home, "quite glad to be / A Frisbee" once again. There is no regret for trying on these other roles; in fact, there is a pleasure in the ability to try them on and decide for himself their inappropriateness. No one else intrudes in this poem to tell the Frisbee he is making a mistake; he makes the determination himself. The home-away-home formula is not one that Silverstein usually uses, instead favoring the home-away-to-heaven-knows-where pattern. But here, the reaffirmation of Frisbeeness, as well as the pleasures of trying on other roles, suggests that children should know their virtues and try other things but find contentment in who they are and what they can do. This is a poem curiously lacking in regret, which Silverstein suggests children need not feel while trying to be other things. The final message is not to be something you're not meant to be, a strong counterstatement of the urge to be anything you want if only you work hard enough. That the Frisbee enjoys flying about is enough satisfaction here. Life is the process, not the destination. Not at least trying alternatives makes for some unsatisfactory endings. "Magic Carpet" (106) suggests the usual imaginative flight pattern but deplores those who use a magic carpet only for a floor covering; obviously, those who stick with the everyday and prosaic miss out on too much.

Avoiding other people's solutions and finding one's own are part of this theme of freedom. "Tryin' on Clothes" (76), discussed earlier, reiterates the theme of being comfortable with who one is, especially in being one with one's own nature and with Mother Nature. In fact, being concerned about clothing and appearances at all is pointedly criticized in another poem, "Outside or Underneath?" (107), in which three characters make decisions about purchasing a wardrobe. The poem points to a false dilemma: Bob buys expensive suits but no underwear, since appearance is what counts to him. Jack buys expensive shorts but wears a ragged suit, since it is what he himself thinks and feels about his invisible underwear that matters to him. Finally, Tom gives no concern to clothes at all and buys "a flute and a box of crayons, / Some bread and cheese and a golden pear." These items, which offer small pleasures and have no value as clothing or coverage, do offer creative possibilities and sensual satisfaction. The joys that a new set of crayons brings, such as the gorgeous precision of their arrangement in a new box and their sharp points and glorious colors, are pleasures of childhood that are particularly piquant and also easily recalled by adults. Although crayons are not exotic, they are exciting, at least when they are new. Cheese and bread are ordinary, though sometimes the two together have romantic connotations for adults. The gold of the pear makes it special and precious as well.

Tom's choice refers to various golden fruits in fairy tales and myths and their great value not only for their jewel-like qualities but also as markers of magic and indicates his singular vision of what is valuable and important. Even the reference to the pear's color as an elegant gold, not simply yellow, marks him as a person of vision and good taste. Tom has the right values; Bob and Jack are dealing with trivialities, whether on the surface or beneath it. Real living is beyond either consideration. Appropriately, this poem has no illustration, since it is not what is visible or even what is hidden that counts.

Parents and Their Uses

Unfortunately, especially for children, freedom has limits, usually imposed by parents. Carrying on in the sly, conniving voice of the trickster, Silverstein suggests to children how they can get what they want from parents in one long, melodramatic poem, "Little Abigail and the Beautiful Pony" (120–21). Abigail is begging her parents for a pony, one of urban children's typical desires in the late twentieth century. Abigail even begs politely, using the word "please." Her parents respond in such accurate parental tones that Silverstein's credibility with a child audience only increases. Her parents retort, "Well, you can't have that pony / But you can have a nice butter pecan / Ice cream cone when we get home." The poet's use of blank verse—or perhaps just the conventions of poetry, short lines divided on the page with no rhyme and no consistent meter—elevates the language by making it appear to be verse, although it is actually the rhythm and diction of everyday speech. The parents' attempt to deflect Abigail's interest in the pony with food, a typical parental ploy, does not work any more than it works with most children beyond early childhood, those old enough to recognize a ploy. Abigail threatens, "If I don't get that pony I'll die," and then proceeds to do just that, in spite of her parents' knowing assertion, "No child ever died yet from not getting a pony." They have dared her, and she has taken the dare. Even Silverstein has taken a dare here; this poem is actually a prose vignette and yet it fits in this volume quite effectively.

The pony is not shown in the illustration, only little Abigail lying on her bed, her parents distraught and tearful on the other page, bemoaning their bad judgment. This is one of the few times that Silverstein uses a true cartoon technique; balloons that contain the parents' words emanate from their mouths. The parents are as sentimental as the poem, so extremely so that it is difficult to take them seriously; this is bathos, not pathos. The mother laments in her cartoon balloon, hand covering her crying eyes, "Oh, if she were only alive I would buy her a hundred ponies!" This is, of course, the vision children have of their own deaths: that they will be sorely missed, perhaps even able to return, and that their parents will be sorry and will give in to every desire. The bathetic tantrum works unequivocally.

Obviously, this poem is so extreme as to be humorous. Like a nineteenth-century consumptive, Abigail wills her own death with such gorgeous theatrics that her parents' reaction is inevitable. The extremity of her thwarted desire and the nearly automatic progress toward her desired resolution, as well as her parents' abject postures at her deathbed, are laughable. Uncharacteristically, Silverstein intrudes at the end of the poem to indicate his intent. This is not a cautionary tale but a useful one, because, as he notes in a stanza in literal parentheses, "(This is a good story / To read to your folks / When they won't buy / You something you want)." The parentheses act as a confidential aside to the child, a code to be eliminated if the poem is ever put to its ostensible use with parents. The frank admission about the need for tools to manipulate parents and the commercial ends of such manipulation bring the poem back into perspective. This is just a game, but Silverstein acknowledges that such games go on between parents and children and that some children can expect better success in getting what they want than the improbable Abigail has had.

The most sadistic poem about parents is "Clarence" (154), who watches commercials on television and believes them. The poem starts out in a direction that seems to suggest that truth in advertising is the theme and that children need to understand the manipulations of marketers. But Silverstein does not at all criticize television or the products sold through it. In fact, the products do exactly what Clarence expects them to. When he sees "A brand-new Maw, a better Paw! / New, improved in every way—" he believes the hype and orders two parents, who arrive by mail. The fate of the old ones is typically suburban: "His old ones he sold at a garage sale," whence they are carted off to hard labor "in an old coal mine."

Once again, the narrator intrudes at the end, this time in the voice of the huckster, who claims that the nagging of demanding parents "simply means they're wearing out"—does this line perhaps beg the question who or what is wearing them out? The quick, clean disposal of the obsolete parents, who toil away at a distance, and the happy conclusion that the new family "all are doing fine" is a vengeance fantasy told in the language of the television age. Novelty, delight in new things, and disinterest in old ones make both sets of parents seem like toys or small appliances, which are summarily replaced. Parents are clearly not fully human, nor are they durable goods, which should be repaired rather than discarded. Like cheap toys, they wear out and should be replaced; the new parents can be enjoyed like a new breakfast cereal. In the illustration, on the far right edge of the right page, the old parents, nearly backing out of the picture, wear an expression of mute, stunned surprise, hardly enough to engender much feeling for them. Like a child on

Christmas, Clarence greets the mailman with glee when the new set of parents arrives in the mailman's sack.

Comic Relief

Of course, the central quality that has kept *Attic* alive and well through several generations of children and adults is the humor. No matter how deftly Silverstein presents his more serious considerations, the book's overriding appeal is its humor and breadth. In its most obvious form, the humor appears as short caricature rhymes. Between "Abigail" and "Clarence," and scattered liberally throughout the volume, are short poems, like limericks, that feature odd people with odd bodies and problems. Many, like Clarence, have names, such as Geraldine, who in "Shaking" (18) tries to create a milk shake by shaking up a cow. "The Sitter" (14) is named Mrs. McTwitter, the *Mc* in her name commonly used to create a humorous title; one recalls Morris McGurk of Dr. Seuss's *If I Ran the Circus* (1956) and *McElligot's Pool* (1947). What comes after the *Mc* is what offers opportunity for rhyme, which in "The Sitter" has a feminine, falling cadence. McTwitter looks a lot like someone who can make such bird noises. She has a pear shape, with an ample posterior for sitting, and a wild-eyed face with a large mass of hair. She looks a lot like Big Bird from *Sesame Street*. Of course, she is as loony as she looks, since her idea of baby-sitting is hatching the baby by sitting on it. Here the baby's feet peek out from under McTwitter's broad hips.

In many of *Attic*'s poems, the point is simply a pun, sometimes one that shows the humorousness and silliness of the subject and its associated actions. For example, "Overdues" (65) features a hunchbacked, balding old man hugging library books that are overdue by 42 years. Does he owe dues on his overdue books? These poems provide spacing and humor throughout the book; like limericks, they describe individuals who are so odd in behavior, appearance, or name as to be humorous. They do not take on large issues or make large points. Sometimes they simply point to some human foible as a source of laughter. Their presence throughout the book provides breaks and quick pacing, since one is not tempted to linger in contemplation of them. Their frequent puns add to the playfulness of language that Silverstein seeks to encourage.

In somewhat longer poems, these personal failings become comic but fatal flaws. Pamela Purse in "Ladies First" (148–49) insists on her precedence as a female. When she is captured by a cannibal who prepares to eat a whole band of children, she insists, "Ladies first" and of course gets her wish. "Almost Perfect" (169) traces the life story of a girl who is hypercritical of birthday parties, the homework of the children she later teaches, and the hugs of otherwise suitable suitors. When she dies at age 98, God pronounces the same verdict on her: "Almost perfect . . . but not quite." Without saying any more, the poet has disposed of her in hell. Barnabus Browning in "Fear" (136) is so fearful of drowning that he drowns in his own overwhelming tears. For these characters, the end is summary death, a satisfying, closed ending to lives not worth preserving or celebrating. In a kind of revenge fantasy, Silverstein satisfactorily disposes of these less-than-fully-human creatures and creates humor at the same time. This is the ultimate punch-line ending—for the character and the reader both.

Silverstein explores the nature and sources of humor in "Cloony the Clown" (74–75), in which Cloony attempts to amuse his circus audience. When he tries to be funny, his audience is distressed; when he relates his own distress, in a long, dramatic monologue to the same audience, they laugh uproariously. He is, of course, frustrated by this odd turn of events, but his conclusion about the sources of humor sounds suspiciously like Silverstein's own: "THAT IS NOT WHAT I MEANT—/ I'M FUNNY JUST BY ACCIDENT." Some of the best humor is unintentional, though even Silverstein would acknowledge that one can put oneself in the way of such humor. Of course, in "Cloony" Silverstein is exploring the Emmet Kelly phenomenon of the sad-faced clown who manages to amuse in spite of his expression and apparent attitude. Oddly enough, this poem does not end with Cloony's discovery of the nature and sources of humor. Rather, everyone laughs at him while "Cloony the Clown sat down and cried."

The final emphasis on disappointment not only begs the question about the feelings of the person who is the butt of a joke but also keeps the poem from being too easy an analysis of humor and its sources. Although "Cloony" might be considered less than successful because it does not end at the climax, the deliberately provocative ending provides the poem with a much richer, more complicated tone than simply ending with Cloony's revelation would have done. Whereas Backwards Bill rides off jauntily into his oppositional life, Cloony the Clown is stuck in the center ring with the difficulties and contradictions in his. "Cloony" is one of the book's longest poems and deals with one of its deeper, more complicated subjects.

Elsewhere, Silverstein is less dramatic in his choice of humorous subjects. He relies on things that interest children, such as dinosaurs and evolution. "Prehistoric" (79) lists the names of various dinosaurs, which are both so difficult for children to pronounce and yet so pleasurable to master—how does one pronounce the *p* in *archaeopteryx,* and what are all those odd, distinctly un-English letter combinations doing in the language? Dinosaurs are monsters that are clearly under children's control because they are extinct. They are not alive even in zoos or in *National Geographic.* The dinosaurs' bony remains provide ghoulish and fascinating reminders about their former existence. Their large, threatening qualities place them in a class with dragons, giants, and other mythical beasts that children obsess about in their fantasies in order to learn imaginative control. *Attic* also contains a poem, appropriately titled "Kidnapped!" (159), a tall tale about being late for school. The reader can only marvel at the glib and breathless pace of the child speaker's complicated excuse for being tardy at school.

Even children's plans that come to naught are the subject of happy poems here. "Rock 'N' Roll Band" (24–25) talks about fame and glory for "seven kids in the sand" who play "homemade guitars and pails and jars." The poem recognizes that the children will not succeed in their dream to become famous and garner admiration from millions. But the illustration below shows the children glorying in the attempt, singing with wide-mouthed voices, lustily if not well, and enjoying the fantasy. The gift of a "Hammock" (10) from grandmother sounds wonderful, but as the child speaker notes, there's no one to help move the trees into the right position. The character who tries to sell "[s]keletons, spirits and haunts" on the "Day after Halloween" (37) gives children a chance to model adult behavior and also a sense of timing. The child in the illustration has several masks on sticks that she hawks with vigor but without much likelihood of success. Facing this poem is one ominously titled "Never" (36), about all the adventures the speaker has not had— no rodeo experiences, no pirate encounters, no card games with lumberjacks, and no rides into the sunset after kissing a girl good-bye. The poem concludes, "Sometimes I get so depressed / 'Bout what I haven't done," mentioning by name an emotion that seldom finds its way into children's poetry but that many children, including most who will read this poem, experience nonetheless.

But is the experience of deflation so devastating? After all, the poem is entertaining in discussing all the experiences a child might consider and amuse himself with if not actually participate in. Writing and imagining are two solutions Silverstein poses for the child as alternatives to both depression and boredom. Even a lowly, discarded "Picture Puzzle Piece" (21) suggests all sorts of possibilities, magical, fantastic, threatening, all of interest. This poem's only illustration is the puzzle piece at the bottom of the page. The poem itself is long and narrow and thus takes up most of the page, leaving little room. Nonillustration is a good choice here. That one can fill up the page and the imagination on one's own is an important message. The stage is set for this poem by one entitled "Signal" (20), on the facing page, about a traffic light that "turns blue / With orange and lavender spots," signaling who knows what for pedestrians and autos. The poem starts with a schoolchild's obedient recitation of what happens when the light is red or green. The other, wilder possibilities open the door for entertaining the ideas in "Picture Puzzle Piece."

Poetic Techniques

The made-up word *burk* points to Silverstein's attitude about the demands of metrics and poetic form. When a rhyme is needed, Silverstein usually goes for the obvious or the convenient rather than straining language or syntax to create an unusual or more appropriate word. When all else fails, the poet is free to make up a word rather than slave over making the poem technically perfect. In fact, the poet need not go to the point of all else failing; children's own nonce words made up to suit the patterns of rhyme and meter in their chants are mimicked here, by a poet who seeks to make poetry easy and fun by taking the easy way out himself. Amusement, rather than innovative poetic expression, is the aesthetic here.

But Silverstein is much more rigorous about the metrics in *Attic* than in *Sidewalk*—he resorts to made-up, forced rhymes less frequently, and in general the rhymes are more precise. Few poems are long enough to warrant stanzas, but those that have them conform to expectations about rhythm, rhyme, and line length established in the first verse paragraph. Silverstein does push the limits of free and blank verse in several poems that pick up the tone of human give-and-take in argument. "The Meehoo with an Exactlywatt" (72) is an extended knock-knock joke inspired by an Abbott and Costello dialogue, as Silverstein notes in his acknowledgments. The dialogue suits the appearance of poetry by providing short exchanges grouped in pairs, an answer that is followed by its questioning response indented below, to form the prose equivalent of a couplet. Italics provide the emphasis needed to bring out the oral qualities of this prose poem and to bring out the exasperation of the meehoo, who has brought his pet exactlywatt for a visit. "Zebra Question" (125) uses this same technique of setting prose on the page like poetry, in paired lines of opposites to mimic the patterns of speech. This is poetry made easy, not just for the poet but for the child reader as well. The poet captures the cadence of everyday speech easily by simply setting it in short lines. Elsewhere, Silverstein uses the relentless rhyming of falling, feminine rhyme words, a typical device of the poet of light verse. "Ations" (59) uses this Latinate suffix to create rhyme words—salutation, consideration, exaggeration, and six others. "Poemsicle" (133) starts with the word "popsicle" and forms other rhymes using the suffix *-sicle*. This kind of rhyme makes the poetry appear effortless and yet humorous in its relentless rhyme pattern, which increases the tension and humor of the punch line at the end. In fact, precise rhyme nearly always guarantees humor here. The precision of the rhyming and metrics is one way in which *Attic* is superior to *Sidewalk* and a greater poetical accomplishment. That Silverstein can also take on global, pensive issues without haranguing or preaching to or boring the child reader simply increases *Attic*'s stature of accomplishment.

The shorter poems in *Attic* use rhyme to lesser effect and rely on illustration more. These are generally the poems that develop from the limerick tradition. Silverstein borrows only the limerick's outward appearance, its subject matter, not its strict metrical form. The short poems, sometimes only four, six, or eight lines long, describe oddball people and are usually accompanied by an illustration. In any case, Silverstein does write with regular meter and reasonably accurate rhyme in the short poems, which only intensifies the humor. But the poems are not so tightly constrained by form that the poet's metrical talents become a focus. The limericks are not virtuoso performances in small form but silly events about silly people.

One innovation that Silverstein uses in his narrative poems is alternate endings. As the master of the punch line and the alternative perspective, Silverstein would naturally find this technique particularly appealing. The result is several opportunities for jokes in the same poem. Silverstein uses this technique most obviously in "Hippo's Hope" (88–89), in which the hippo attempts to fly by putting on wings and proceeding to the edge of a cliff. The poem offers three different endings, each one stanza long, on the succeeding page. They are parenthetically labeled for the reader's understanding of the technique: "(Happy ending)" shows the hippo succeeding, "(Unhappy ending)" shows him at the bottom of the cliff, and "(Chicken ending)" shows him deciding to have a snack instead of trying to fly at all. The attenuation of the ending through three different perspectives increases the humor; so do the meaningful words incorporated into the scat song refrains. For example, "high," "fly," and "bye" all combine with the repeated "hi-dee" rhyme in the happy ending, and "bones," "moans," and "groans" with the "hi-dee" in the unhappy ending: "Bye-hi-dee-boop" and "groans-hi-dee-glop" are two examples. That the poet can instill meaning in nonsense shows his technical control over his humor.

Illustrational Techniques

Elsewhere in *Attic*, the endings are apparent only in the illustration. "Have Fun" (144–45) is a four-line poem that guarantees the absence of sharks at a park pool; no humor is apparent in this poem until the viewer notes the octopus below water level. "Buckin' Bronco" (62–63) promises a bad joke and a rough ride, as the horse is pictured nearly upside down, posterior foremost. The first speaker invites someone to ride this violent beast, detailing the rough quality of the ride in the first three stanzas. Another speaker picks up the dare in the last stanza and seems assured, at least briefly. Whereas all the other stanzas are five lines long, this last one is a short three and a half, as the rider is verbally and visually tossed out of the poem. The last line, "Here is me," is followed by an arrow pointing to two flying boots exiting off the page on the upper right side.

Some poems comment visually, though not verbally, on each other, linked by an illustration or more usually by two illustrations, in which the figures make eye contact or cast a glance across a two-page spread that the viewer's eye follows. The most humorous of these illustrations is of the tormented person in "Unscratchable Itch" (52), whose hands cannot reach down his back to reach the spot they need to. Across the page, a little waifish girl offers her hand up toward the spot. However, the end of her poem reveals what her gesture means. "Squishy Touch" (53) is about the Midas touch that turns everything to "raspberry jello." A decomposing pile of victims melts under her feet, a face in profile and a foot still visible in the wiggly mass. The little girl's hand outstretched in the illustration at the end of the poem offers a threat rather than help to the one with the unscratchable itch. The onomatopoeia at the end of every line describing the effects of the touch make this poem delightfully disgusting. As mother disappears with a "(gloosh)" after an unfortunate kiss, the open hand offers a "(sklush)" to the man with his itch.

The unity across the two-page spreads and the great detail in them, especially as compared to the illustrations in *Sidewalk*, give the reader a more pleasing, more organized experience. These are poems designed to go together, and the book appears less an anthology and more of a varied, though thoughtfully organized, experience. Although the book's overall effect is humorous and although it is the humorous experiences that the child reader remembers, this is not just a collection of illustrated jokes in verse. The book succeeds because of the rhythm of the variety, but it is not a scattershot experience. Although it breaks new ground in its topics of sexiness versus decency, depression, and disposal of undesirable parents, it is so pleasing an experience for children that the pleasure is what remains. Few of the poems are so referential as to require explication or explanation of allusion: one need not know about the Cyclops or Emmet Kelly to understand these poems thoroughly. All the poems' easy accessibility makes the book an easy read for most children.

Yet it is this success in treating these unmentionable topics that many parents and teachers object to. Like a banned book, Silverstein succeeds precisely by offending the keepers of propriety and respectability. He explores topics that have long been the common parlance of childhood, though they have not previously been explored in poetry. For some time, Silverstein's choice of topics succeeded in keeping his poetry in the hands of children but out of the classroom and off the library shelves. But rather than censoring and thereby increasing this book's appeal, teachers and parents have relented and duly admitted Silverstein to the classroom and the home as an introduction to the pleasure of poetry, even at their own expense, as teachers and parents are often the butts of the jokes. As a truth teller about childhood's conditions in the late twentieth century, Silverstein has found acceptance among his dual audiences, both adult and youthful, and in his success and daring in this book has offered these audiences a common meeting ground. As I argue in the last chapter, Shel Silverstein's poetry, at its zenith in *Attic*, may be the last best hope to encourage Americans to read other American poetry.

Chapter Five

The Geometry of
Human Relationships

Both *The Missing Piece* (1976) and *The Missing Piece Meets the Big O* (1981) have geometric forms as characters. They have their origin in a poem in *Attic,* "Shapes" (77), which tells the story of a square who, characteristic of his shape, sits still. Suddenly a triangle swoops down from nowhere and stabs the square in the back. A circle rolls by and takes the square to the hospital, the triangle still stuck in his back. Although the poem is oddly violent, the point is really the three shapes' personification and their human interaction. The three shapes are shown in the illustration with smiling faces and eyes, the square and triangle on top of the circle, which rolls off to the hospital apparently in no pain; similarly, this rollicking little rhyme rolls on with no particular point except to generate interest in the plot's personification of its raw materials. The effect is similar to that of a nursery rhyme: the poem moves so quickly that motivation for action and consequent pain do not receive consideration. Action and the related joys found in motion are the main focus.

Silverstein published *The Missing Piece* and *The Missing Piece Meets the Big O* closely after each of the successful poetry volumes, *Where the Sidewalk Ends* and *A Light in the Attic.* Both *The Missing Piece* and *Big O* maintain the appearance of a Silverstein poetry volume, though each deals with an adult theme. Children are most likely to read these books because of their similar appearance to other Silverstein books—they have white covers with black lettering, simple line illustrations, and the characteristic binding with the author's signature on the cover and dust jacket. Children may not notice that these books have adult themes but instead take the simple text and illustrations at face value; they appear to be picture books about traveling and friendships on the road. As one reviewer points out, the books' more disturbing messages will likely escape most children.[1] The dust-jacket copy for *The Missing Piece* claims that the book's theme is "the nature of quest and fulfillment."[2] Although this encompasses part of the book's message, its more central issue is the nature of relationships and their relative importance in an

individual's life. *Big O* continues the theme by investigating the nature
of personal responsibility for happiness in life.

The Missing Piece is not really about the missing piece, who is a secondary character; rather, it is about a creature shaped like a Pac-Man—
it is round and shown only in profile; its eye and wedge-shaped mouth
are its sole anatomical features. Oddly, though this character is
described as neuter and appears round and feminine, it is apparently
male, on the move and on the prowl, looking for an ideal mate. The
wedge shape, even though it is more phallic, is the apparent female. The
Pac-Man's characteristic mode of locomotion is to roll, which the round
character does with some difficulty because of the wedge it is missing—
the missing piece for which it searches. The missing piece is what it
seeks to fit into its mouth to complete its circle and make it perfectly
round, more easily rolled. It notices its incompleteness on the first page:
"It was missing a piece. And it was not happy."

To seek completeness, the round shape sets off on a journey, seeming
anything but unhappy and dissatisfied. On the journey, it sings a song
with a rollicking rhythm and a jiving refrain, either "Hi-dee-ho, here I
go" or "So grease my knees and fleece my bees / I'm lookin' for my
missin' piece." The refrain sounds like the scat rhyming of a typical folk
song, some of which have such nonsense syllables as "doo-dah" or
"derry-derry-down"; Silverstein's nonsense also has the beat and rhythm
of one of Silverstein's own musical compositions, which are both country
-and-western and rock-and-roll in character.

Along the journey, the round figure stops to chat with a worm, smell
a flower, and flirt and play with a butterfly. When the butterfly lands on
its head, decorating it and pleasing it, "this was the best time of all."
This scene appears at first to be the story's climax, but this is not the
end. Not content to remain in this happiest of situations, the shape
moves on and meets various pieces, most wedge shaped, that appear to
be its missing piece. But all have various deficiencies: one is too independent to belong to anyone else and sounds like a strident feminist; one is
too small; one is too large; one is just right, but the circle does not know
how to hold on gently enough, so the piece breaks. Finally the circle
finds a willing, fitting piece and continues its journey completed in
shape and apparently now whole. Again, it would seem that the story
has come to a climax.

But the complications of such completeness appear immediately:
now that the perfectly round, completed shape can roll quickly, it has no
time to observe the sights it passes or the worm or butterfly or flower;

its creativity is also hampered because, with the newly found piece stuffed in its mouth, it cannot sing. With the piece in its mouth, the song becomes garbled: "So krease ny meas / An bleez ny drees / Uf frown. . . ." The word "frown," its best attempt at saying "found" with its mouth full, points the way to the ending. The success of having found the piece causes a frown, not satisfaction. The circle gently sets the piece down and rolls away; the piece, on the left side of the page, looks poignantly at the circle, which rolls along to the far right and takes up the earlier song: "I'm lookin' for my missin' piece." The butterfly again lights on its nose, and no words in the text comment. The book continues with two consecutive two-page spreads that show only an empty landscape and the butterfly flitting playfully on the penultimate two-page spread, the author's way of suggesting that perhaps the end of the story is simply more landscape to cover, more events—holes, blizzards, insects, and oceans—to experience.

It is clear that to the author, relationships are fine as long as they are not inhibiting; in fact, commitment, although satisfying in its completeness, is also stifling of certain other pleasures, such as creativity, travel, and involvement with others besides the partner. Like all pleasures of life, that of commitment is fleeting though powerful in its satisfaction and realization. At the risk of pun, surely invited by the author's other accomplishments and by his choice of a circle as the story's main character, one could conclude that the highest value in life is to rock and roll, sing and move, enjoy the pleasures, including relationships, along the way. But stasis, even at a point of fulfillment, will not satisfy forever, and obligations to others encumber mobility. Echoing "The Search" (166), at the end of *Sidewalk*, the author here concludes that restlessness and pleasures only of the moment, not the stasis of wholeness and completeness, are the real interests in life. Life is to be lived in its process, not its destinations.

If the story seems reminiscent of other Silverstein parables, most especially *The Giving Tree*, it is because the author, in this book's expansive, nearly blank pages and spare text, nearly demands that the knowledgeable reader invest the characters and events with adages and characterizations borrowed from elsewhere to complete the story's sense and meaning. For example, when the circle climbs the mountain, only to roll back down it on the next page, the informed reader recalls Sisyphus, doomed for life to roll a rock to the summit of a mountain, only to have it fall back down again. The various meteorological events in *The Missing Piece*—snow, rain, sun—recall the postal carrier's pledge to deliver the mail no matter what the weather. And the journey over various oceans and terrains, including jungles, recalls all those famous voyagers and explorers in history and in literature who quest to achieve some goal—Noah, Odysseus, Columbus, Robinson Crusoe. The circle's act of stopping to smell a flower reminds the reader of the adage in the 1970s that one should stop and smell the roses, to enjoy life rather than hurry through it, as well as the older carpe diem theme of enjoying life and youth while one can. Even the idea of two human beings merging their complementary shapes in a sexual act has mythic origins, in primitive folk stories. By making such indirect references, Silverstein enlarges the story for the more sophisticated reader while keeping it simple for the less well read, such as children.

Indeed, the shapes themselves nearly demand commentary. Their sexuality is clear to those even minimally skilled in Freudian criticism. The pointed wedge/triangle and the wedge-shaped receptacle of a mouth need no more sexual explication than simply pointing to them; the pleasurable, sensual aspects of the two parts coming together is underscored by their reaction to their union, a nearly wordless "Hummm?" "Ummmm!" The extra *m* on the response to the question—which shape is saying which line is not clear—expresses quite subtly that the respondent experiences even greater pleasure than does the questioner. The fit is pleasurable and perfect, like a deep kiss or perhaps a sexual act. Perhaps the circle is female and the missing piece, phallic in shape, is male, though "on the road" stories about women are few.

But roundness achieved by closing the circle has meanings other than sexual ones. The image of completeness and wholeness transcends physical connotations. Being a complete circle suggests such qualities as being well rounded, flexible, easy to move, like a wheel, capable of accommodating with minimal bumps and chips. It is the ideal shape, one of stability, unity, constancy, and eternity. Its bouncinesss contrasts markedly to the wedge or triangle, which cannot move as well; triangles suggest stability, like a pyramid, but not movement. Silverstein's cleverness is evident in his ability to give both wedge and circle personalities and various meaningful expressions by slight variations in the placement of the eye, the tilt of the circle, and slight contortions of the wedge.

The Missing Piece is a story of its age, the 1970s. With the hippie counterculture extolling the virtues of pleasure, of living life to its fullest, of relationship without commitment, and ultimately of freedom to do whatever gives pleasure, *The Missing Piece* continues the *Playboy* doctrine of the fun of sex and the avoidance of permanence and commitment because of their limitations. Flower children, later called the "me" generation, sought to break away from the stultifying assumptions about family life and embraced the acceptability of extramarital sexual relationships. Smelling flowers, enjoying nature, and moving on to new adventures and experiences all characterize the 1990s, in which the more conservative values of family, marriage, and stability have been reinforced by the threats of AIDS and international political and economic instability. The "nature of the quest" that the dust jacket of *The Missing Piece* promises as the book's focus is not so central. Rather, the all-importance of the quest itself and its process is the real message. Moving on, no matter where, is better than the happiest moments of stasis in this book. Somehow, all pleasure is ephemeral, ultimately unsatisfying. Only in moving, in the process of the quest, does one find happiness. Transcendent happiness subsists in seeking to find it. Certainly the book's joys of singing and motion will appeal to children, but this is not a Silverstein story that wears its age well. The book's focus on the nature of relationships is also typical of Silverstein. Being ready to bolt, avoiding even healthy interdependence and any obligation, is highly commended here.

The book's companion piece is *The Missing Piece Meets the Big O* (1981), published five years later. This time, the title more accurately describes the book's content; the story actually does concentrate on the missing piece, the wedge shape, as the protagonist. In this case, the piece seems to be more clearly female, decorating itself with flowers to be more attractive, trying to attract Pac-Man-shaped round partners rather than chasing after them. It is more phallic than the circles in appearance but not in behavior. The shape's stability here, with its baseline and low center of gravity, is an asset—it cannot move on its own by rolling, or so it assumes, at least at the beginning. It simply sits alone waiting for a mate who can take it up, perhaps swallow it up, to help it move. The opening page shows it resting on one side, looking from the far right of the page toward the left, a characteristically unprogressive stance in a picture book, in which the story and the illustration usually move from left to right. There is no future in this leftward stance, no action; the missing piece will have to learn to move or let the action pass it by. Once again the emphasis is on movement as the highest value.

Fortunately, some possible suitors do come along, though at first only bad fits. The bad fit or inappropriate shape usually implies a character defect—the dummies don't even know to take the piece into the correct orifice. The squares are not only geometrically wrong for rolling, they're also square, suggesting too conservative or too traditional a mind-set. The one possible partner who puts the wedge on a pedestal and then abandons it obviously has a peculiar view of what wedges want and what they are for. The collectors have too many pieces. The deficient, who appear somehow damaged, have too many orifices for one piece to fill. Finally, there are the Pac-Man characters, a herd of hungry circles with mouths for eating missing pieces, not for helping them or for achieving mutual completeness with them. As the piece becomes disappointed in not finding its mate, it tries various feminine tactics, such as decorating itself with flowers to become more attractive and calling attention to itself with a large, Las Vegas-like neon sign, which perhaps suggests, ever so gently, the desperate act of prostitution in order to find a partner.

Finally, the ideal partner comes along and the two roll off together in a perfect blissful embrace; both wedge and circle close their eyes in contentment. But as in *Missing Piece,* this first ending is false. Almost immediately, the missing piece begins to grow, so much that it outgrows the fit. Of course, the circle moves on, singing the song from the earlier book with one significant modification: "I'm lookin' for my missin' piece, one that won't increase." The stability of a relationship, Silverstein seems to imply, depends on partners not changing too much; it is more likely, however, that one partner will grow, mature, or perhaps just simply change because of the relationship, even though the growth is detrimental to the partners' fit.

Then the Big O finally appears; it is larger than the other circles and has no missing wedge, no needs, and no expectations of the missing piece. Although the larger O suggests completeness and wisdom, the wedge shape unfortunately still identifies itself as someone's missing piece; it needs someone else to be complete and is incapable of moving by itself. But in a motion described as "liftpullflopliftpullflop,"[3] the wedge finally begins to move, wearing away its edges and angles and by implication its imperfections—the chips on its shoulder, the character flaws that limit it. Gradually it attains a circular shape, moving fast enough to catch up with the Big O. On the last page, the former wedge and the Big O move together side by side, the smaller, new O humbled by but in comfortable companionship with the Big O, who appears to be a mentor to the former wedge.

The wedge's character is clearer than that of the Big O. Obviously the name O comes from its shape, but the Big O might also represent the Big Zero or even the all-encompassing Big Everything. The concept of completeness here seems Zen-like, a melding of yin and yang, male and female, all and nothing at the same time. The Big O's wisdom is suggested not only by its size but also by its gentle advice and willingness to move on without false sentiment. Life flows for the Big O, smoothly and with little upset. Again, relationships are valuable but are not life's most important value, which seems once again to be moving along. The terrain here is less important than in *The Missing Piece;* here the shapes' interactions and characters define the plot. Silverstein uses more text to explain the plot; this is a more wordy book than the other, though it is also a calmer book because of the Big O's presence.

Although both books are dated, this one is the less successful of the two, depending as it does more on authorial intrusion to spell out meaning and less on the epic suggestiveness and allusions to other literature that characterize the first book. On the other hand, *The Big O's* final message, to look inside oneself for the resources one needs to succeed in life, seems more appropriate to children. It closely parallels the message of L. Frank Baum's *Wizard of Oz* (1900), one that most readers find quite satisfying: the scarecrow, the tin woodsman, and the lion all find the virtues that they need to succeed in their quest, and Dorothy has the power to return to her home with her all the time, though she does not know it. Certainly these messages of self-sufficiency are appropriate for children, though in Silverstein's book the messages are delivered in a story that has sexual dimensions. Though the book talks a great deal about the relations between the sexes, it is less marked by the *Playboy* philosophy of "love them and leave them" and more informed by the transcendent values of self-assurance and resourcefulness.

For those who enjoy *The Giving Tree*, the parables of growth, self-reliance, and independence in relationships in *The Missing Piece* and *The Missing Piece Meets the Big O* will have appeal. Those predisposed to reading these stories as gentle parables of maturity and creativity, of wholeness and neediness, will find them satisfying. These books make it easy to moralize without having to achieve any great feats of literary criticism. Children will find the books attractive because of the simple, childlike illustrations that nearly tell the story on their own.

For those who probe more deeply, the stories can be disturbing; for the happily married, the stories will be objectionable at least. Although these books succeed, they are much less provocative and complicated than *The Giving Tree*, much less childlike and silly than the picture books for children. They appear to be novel length but are really extended picture books, although they have none of the complex color illustrations that contemporary picture books for children do. More like easy readers, they provide another glimpse into Silverstein's skill as a storyteller and fabulist. And once again, the author's refusal to end the books, his skill in violating expectations, and his multiple levels of meaning will attract readers who admire the books but do not quite understand all that they imply. In contrasting these books with the poetry volumes that they both follow, it becomes clear that the anthology, not the picture book, even in an extended format, is Silverstein's most successful venue, and the older child, not both children and adults, is his best audience.

Chapter Six
The Poet's Place

Poetry has long been one of the great unexplored areas in children's literature. Few reputations, of either poets or critics, have been built on it, since most acclaim and notice goes to novels. What criticism exists for poetry derives in many cases from the "beauties" school of criticism—pointing out the poetry's beauties, such as a poet's or a line's excellence, without any particular explanation of wherein the beauty lies. The reasons for this neglect of children's poetry are twofold: first, except for the most simple rhymes, the American population has a general distaste for poetry, a result of the second reason, the unfortunate way in which poetry is introduced to children in school. Poetry has for some time had to be taught to children, especially since it has lost its currency with the general reading public by becoming increasingly obscure and unavailable to any but the most poetically literate. Poetry has lost its audience because of the hard work it takes to understand both its form and its content.

The result is that children first meet up with poetry in school, where it is presented in a pedagogical, systematic way, with emphasis on the poems' literary and didactic values. In fact, since Isaac Watts, children's poetry has been, in the main, designed to preach. Most children, and most adults as well, realize that the poetry introduced at school is designed to propagandize manners and values that are predominantly Protestant and puritanical. In fact, from the seventeenth century to the present, the didactic mode of children's poetry has been the only justification that most educational theorists have been able to find for presenting it to children. The entertainment value, if any, was clearly and distantly secondary. Poetry has had "spinach" value—good for you but with little appeal to the palate. No one particularly thought to teach children how to enjoy poetry, thereby lessening its appeal even further. So teaching poetry has had a double detriment: it has conveyed the message that, first, poetry is difficult and cannot be understood without extraordinary linguistic tools and skills, and second, it cannot be enjoyed.

Perry Nodelman has admitted that, for all of us who do not read poetry regularly, the life untouched by poetry can be perfectly satisfying.

116

Poetry has no minimum daily requirement; one's life is not deficient because one does not enjoy reading it. America's founding fathers, especially Thomas Jefferson, insisted that citizens of a democracy needed to be literate in order to function responsibly, but such literacy did not necessarily demand poetic sensibility. On the other hand, Nodelman says that many more people would enjoy poetry if only they knew how. He points to those schoolchildren who read poetry without instruction on what and how to enjoy as being ill served.[1] Thankfully, Nodelman has nonetheless entered the void and begun teaching the pleasure in poetry that has long been neglected.

Fortunately, readers of Silverstein's poetry need no such compensatory education, and that is one of the beauties of *Sidewalk* and *Attic*: no special tools of interpretation, either for the pictures or for the poetry, are necessary. Although the volumes may have richer meaning and experience for those who understand poetic and illustrational techniques, Silverstein's poems are immediate enough that they carry plenty of weight and pleasure without the other knowledge in hand.

In his book *Can Poetry Matter?*, Dana Gioia likewise decries the distance between poetry and everyday readers but points to the success of regional poets in speaking to their audiences and attracting a readership. A regional poet's ability to speak using the diction that his audience understands, to choose topics in which the audience has particular interest and understanding of, to write about everyday occurrences in a natural, poetic way, serve both the poet and the audience well. Because the regional poet does not attract national or literary interest, the intensely loyal following of his readers is not well known to literary professionals, nor is the regional poet's distinctive success realized beyond the region. Outsiders frequently just don't get it.

Although Gioia speaks mainly of Midwesterner Ted Kooser as his exemplar regional poet,[2] all the guidelines that he sets for judging a regional poet a success can be applied to Silverstein, a kind of regional poet whose audience is children in the lower elementary and middle school grades, the region of childhood before adolescence. Silverstein does not expect to speak to a general audience of readers of all ages or even to children in general. If he succeeds with adults, it is because these adults remain actively connected to the child of the age and sophistication that Silverstein has targeted. One of Gioia's statements about Kooser could also apply to Silverstein: "There is little in Kooser's work that would summon forth a great performance. There are no problems to solve, no dazzling bravado passages to master for the dexterous critic eager to earn an extra curtain call. .... [T]here is little a critic can provide that the average reader cannot, because the difficulties . . . are experiential rather than textual" (p. 95). Both Silverstein and Kooser, who do not provide anything for professional critics to latch onto, have attracted their audiences as champions.

Yet Gioia is not without standards to judge poetry's success; even the successful Kooser can fall short occasionally, as can Silverstein. But Gioia's guidelines are fair and sensible and give a handle on how to judge an individual poet's works. The poet's originality, not necessarily of poetic technique but perhaps of topic and voice, the scope of the volume and its integrity as a whole, and the poet's clear sense of addressing a specific audience are Gioia's standards, as are the number of perfect poems and the variety of the voice (pp. 97–98). There are admitted failures in Silverstein's volumes of poetry, as noted in chapters 3 and 4. But there are also those excellent models that are perfect, in expression, diction, word choice, and sometimes even meter, also noted in those chapters.

Finally, it is Silverstein's choice of topics and range of voices that establish his place among poets for children; he has been recognized even among literary professionals for his staying power and popular appeal. His topics are sometimes unspeakable but are certainly thinkable, and Silverstein has succeeded in Alexander Pope's poetic criterion of saying in poetry what is universally thought but nowhere else expressed so well. The voice in the poem "Whatif" (90), from *Attic*, about the negative possibilities that children are free to consider only during the dark night of the soul and only when they are alone, is one of Silverstein's most potent. Silverstein takes on the voice of the older child considering what might happen to him in the case of certain bad events, some of which are major traumas, such as parental divorce, others of which are less large but no less significant and frightening to a child, such as green chest hair. In "Listen to the Mustn'ts" (27), from *Sidewalk*, Silverstein takes on the avuncular voice of an adult advisor, encouraging a child in the face of all the social etiquette that limits him; the unclelike voice seeks to free the child's imagination, to let the mind's possibilities range freely. These are two of the more serious and successful poems in the volumes, but Silverstein also manages a range of other voices and topics that reliably succeeds in capturing what schoolchildren think about and how they express it—everything short of the swearing and obscenity that would call down the censors' and other adults' opprobrium.

It is Silverstein's subversion of topic that captures Alison Lurie's attention and commendation. Silverstein's subversion is part of his popular success, although it has mitigated literary recognition of his works. Literary critics continue to devote their attention to a canon of poetry that has messages and techniques acceptable to critics, teachers, parents, and other adults. But there are those books that Lurie calls "sacred texts of childhood," those works she would therefore call "great" because they "express ideas and emotions not generally approved of or even recognized at that time; they make fun of honored figures and piously held beliefs; and they view social pretenses with clear-eyed directness, remarking—as in Andersen's famous tale—that the emperor has no clothes."[3]

Silverstein tells the truth to children, right down to the messy, open, inconclusive endings and occasional sentimentality. He debunks fantasy happy endings as lying to children and inculcates self-reliance as the best protection against life and guarantee of success in it.[4] In his wish-fulfillment poems, about disposing of annoying siblings and parents and about manipulating parents, he gives voice to children's unspoken thoughts and sometimes becomes the subjects of children's private conversations. Silverstein's ideas have seldom before become subjects of poetry and are certainly not ideas that adults discuss without preachy rejoinder. But in such poems as "For Sale" (*Sidewalk*, 52) and "Clarence" (*Attic*, 154), about disposing of siblings and parents, Silverstein enters the fantasy so completely, with such gusto and approval, that the child readers learn to trust the poet and entwine themselves in the experience of the poetry. In Silverstein's advice poems, which are few but nonetheless genuine, he has the readers' trust so thoroughly that the didacticism is likely to be taken to heart rather than scoffed at for being treacly. Silverstein follows in the tradition of Isaac Watts in this infrequent educational mode and follows eighteenth-century assumptions about children's poetry both delighting and teaching, yet Silverstein's teaching is infrequent enough and the lessons taught so easily embraced that the primary motive never seems pedagogical.

Above all, Silverstein renders pleasure to the reader; that is the primary motive behind his poetry, and in it he succeeds. At the beginning of Perry Nodelman's book on understanding children's literature, aptly titled *The Pleasures of Children's Literature*, he gives a long list of pleasures that literature for children can give.[5] On these counts, Silverstein renders full measure. The jokes are frequent and ribald enough to keep the reader's attention, yet the book is segmented into two-page spreads so that the reader avoids a surfeit of humor. *Sidewalk* and *Attic* need not be read continuously, from front to back, but can be sampled, placed aside, and reentered at almost any point. The reader need not put forth much effort to enjoy these books, and the enjoyment is fulsome regardless of the effort. The illustrations are both a lure and a gift from the illustrator; as discussed earlier, they, too, are easily enjoyed, and the code of the cartoon—quick, radiating lines that indicate motion, movement primarily from left to right to encourage forward motion, and few symbols, mostly faces and action with little background—simply supports the book's rapid, pleasurable pace. The easiness of reading both poetry and illustration also underscores the author's overall approach to life—easy, full of motion and progress, with short stops along the way to enjoy the view.

The physical appearance of these volumes simply encourages their easy pleasure. No cheap knockoffs in paperback have appeared. Both *Sidewalk* and *Attic* are still constructed of the same high-quality materials used for the first issue, with gold leaf on the spine and the author's signature on the cover. But this cover is seldom seen, since the dust jackets, with their distinctive white background and black illustration and lettering, mark a Silverstein volume with his signature design. The volume of poetry without its dust jacket simply does not appear to be authentic Silverstein. The heavy paper stock makes page turning easy, and the generous white space, between poems, between poems and illustrations, even between individual letters, makes the book a gift for the eye. A book like this is hard to lose and easy to treasure. It is definitely made for keeping when not in use and unlikely to be discarded, either unwittingly or deliberately—this is not a book one is likely to be done with permanently.

Silverstein fails as a technical poet for a reason: he invites the child, as the poet's equal, to join in a poetic moment. In order to do so, the poet must use language and poetic form that a child can recognize. As X. J. Kennedy and Dorothy M. Kennedy note, old-fashioned patterns of rhythm, rhyme, and sound dominate even the most contemporary children's poetry. It is as if "shaken only a little by those winds of change that in the 1960s and 1970s swept the mainland of American literature, poetry for children today seems an offshore island doing its best to stay serene" with poetic devices clearly antiquated in poetry for adults.[6] If Silverstein pushes the limits of topics and voice, he wisely avoids pushing the limits of poetry and technique.

It seems likely that Silverstein knew instinctively those qualities that research shows children most prefer in poetry. Two studies, one a survey of the research, the other a survey of children, show that the qualities children like best in poetry are identifiable rhythm, rhyme, and sound patterns. But even more telling than the poetic devices is the poems' tone. Children's overwhelming preference, as reported in the research, is for humor in poems.[7] Here Silverstein succeeds without question, even among adult professional literary critics. Such words as "uproarious," "zany," and even the more tepid "delightful" dominate the reviews of both *Attic* and *Sidewalk*.

What's New

After Silverstein's absence of more than 20 years, *Falling Up* appeared on bookstore shelves as a surprise.[8] Twenty years is several generations in children's literature, and the reading public for children's poetry during this time habituated itself to the kinds of poetry that Silverstein had originated and popularized earlier. In fact, other poets carried Silverstein's tradition of the gross and disgusting in verse even further and kept current with new inventions and gadgets and language in the popular culture of kid life that formed the basis of Silverstein's early success. After 20 years, the scatological joking found in *Falling Up* has become common, and as noted earlier, Silverstein's books have begun to show their age. As a result the bawdy and bathroom humor in *Falling Up* now seems tame and almost nonchalant.

Much of what is new in *Falling Up* has to do with poetry about new gadgetry, especially that unavailable to the poet earlier. This is Silverstein catching up with 20 years of technology. Thus there is a poem about using a computer in the writing process, "Writer Waiting" (58). The computer's promise to make writing easier through word processing, however, has no merit unless the poet has a topic, something to write about; the computer fails to generate writing on its own, and the writer using the computer in the poem finds himself with low-tech writer's block. As most adults and children know, only a human can make a computer work, and finding inspiration to write is not easier because of new technology. Thus Silverstein ends the poem typically—a great work is promised while the writer sits at the keyboard, but the punch line is that he can find nothing to write about.

As might easily be expected, there are also poems about the ubiquitous use of electricity to power children's amusement, and there is even a poem about a Walkman and its uses and abuses. "Headphone Harold" (161) is one of Silverstein's peculiarly obsessive children, who insists on walking on the railroad tracks while listening to the radio through his headphones. His doom is obvious—he cannot hear the train coming.

Even the TV remote control gets a poem; "Remote-a-Dad" (112) suggests using this dandy appliance to control fathers, the ultimate command being "off," which extinguishes them. The overloading of circuits powering household entertainment and appliances also gets a poem, "Plugging In" (8). The punch line of the tripped circuit breaker seems inevitable, given the long list of electrical implements the family seems to be using at once.

Silverstein even occasionally flirts with the political issues of the nineties, though he nowhere pursues them as seriously as he does the issues of the seventies in the earlier volumes. In "Description" (78) children vehemently debate about what God looks like. One insists he is black; another, a girl, insists he is a she. But in this poem, which is a series of one-liners, the punch line belongs to the speaker, who claims to have God's own handwriting sample—unlikely though that may seem. The issue about God's appearance is muted by the preposterous, unexplored issue of having God's autograph at all.

There is a poem about animal rights, "Warmhearted" (59), about a woman who wears a fox stole that is still alive. The live fox around the matron's neck looks put upon but does not appear to be truly suffering. Nowhere in this book is there the persisting, moving poetry, like that found in the earlier volumes, about the political and philosophical issues that now preoccupy Silverstein. The old causes seem to have been resolved, and the new ones are treated less seriously and less extensively.

Instead, there is a pattern of poems about issues that seem typical of an older, gentler poet, one who is considering his advancing age. Even some of the obvious jokes seem more typical of an older person than in tune exclusively with children. For instance, the book's sixth poem, "Scale" (8), is about someone who is overweight, especially around the middle. He is sure that the scale he is standing on would speak reassuringly to him if only he could see it over his spare tire. The person on the scale is not an oddball character or even a pudgy child; this distribution of weight around the middle is typical of the middle aged and older. Although children will laugh at this poem, its target audience is more likely the middle aged and lumpy.

Some of the poems start by celebrating children's natural tendencies but at the end make concessions to adults rather than indulging nature inordinately or punishing adults. The most obvious of these is "Noise Day" (26–27), about a national celebration set aside for children to make their loudest, most irritating and disruptive sounds with as much abandon as they can muster. The poem is a particularly joyful and successful one, with its catalog of all the sounds that children can make, such as dribbling a bowling ball or slamming a door. But the poem ends unexpectedly with an adult's negotiated settlement. These noises can go on all day, but "[t]he rest of the days—be *quiet* please." A younger Silverstein would have encouraged the children to keep it up until the adults were driven crazy. This is the voice of limited indulgence and adult need for peace and quiet, in spite of the fact that, with the exception of the last line, the poem celebrates childhood's exuberance.

Similarly, *Falling Up* contains two poems on old age that are the closest to the successful serious poems of the earlier volumes. "Stork Story" (166–70) suggests the process of reincarnation. As the stork delivers babies, so it takes old people away "[w]hen it's their time to go." At their destination, an unspecified location, all their ailments are removed from them; their bodies are reconditioned, their brains are restored to the blankness of childhood, and then the stork takes them back to life as babies. This is a comforting image of death, one that does not press a particular theological point about dying but simply reassures a child reader, or a reader of any age, that dying is not something to be feared. The imagery is more reminiscent of a garage or a recycling center than of a hospital or of heaven, and the reconditioning happens painlessly and without sorrow. That the end is the beginning is also a typical Silverstein reversal. And yet this poem breaks new ground for Silverstein in that it treats the serious subject of death with a light touch but with dignity and without uproar.

Another poem about the aging process, "The Folks Inside" (144), explains to children that they, too, will age and that their potential to become old people is latent in them; it's just a matter of time until "[t]hose old folks / Down inside you / Wake up . . . and come out to play." One wonders if Silverstein senses his own aging and mortality. Certainly the dust-jacket photo shows a more pensive, more accessible poet than do the earlier photos; his hands are folded in front of him in a restful, perhaps even prayerful attitude, his eyes making clear contact with the viewer. This is not the kicking, sneering musician or the reluctant, casual poet of the earlier dust jackets. The poet in this portrait is accessible, seemingly more gentle and quiet both inside and outside this book.

The illustrations have become both more adventurous and more problematic. In his attempt to unify each page's layout by placing the illustrations across a two-page spread, Silverstein occasionally puts the illustration's focal point in the gutter, something that beginning illustration students learn not to do in their first week of class. Overall, the drawing style has not evolved, and Silverstein still has some lessons to learn. On the other hand, there is an illustration on the end page, glued to the cover on the right-hand side, truncated at the gutter: two legs with shoes, the rest of the body lost in the gutter. These legs do, in fact, look as though they are falling, perhaps up, continuing the title even at the end of the book as a design element that demonstrates Silverstein's continuing unconventionality about illustration and what constitutes the illustrator's space. The artist's potential to joke seems much broader than earlier. Some illustrations reappear, with modification. The little bare man who traipses across the last page of *Sidewalk* and then trails his beard behind him through the index of the same book reappears here across the bottoms of the index pages with a placard in hand, which reads "One more time." The two masks, happy and sad, from *Attic* reappear at the top of the index page, this time on children's heads. The children, a boy and a girl, round faced and startled in expression, wear the masks like hats with the visors up. Here we have both the old and the new brought together. One poem, on page 98, "Allison Beals and her Twenty-Five Eels," even makes an illustrational reference to a poem on page 59. The eels and their uses are disposed of effectively, except for the one in the last line: "And one got a new job on page fifty-nine." A quick turn back to page 59 shows that this eel functions as a power cord to a computer, its mouth open as if it were going to bite the outlet. Is this an electric eel? On the whole, Silverstein works harder here to tie the illustrations in with earlier works and with other poems.

One of the other 24 eels that accompany Allison through life demonstrates one of the most significant changes in the book's overall tone and conduct, though this significance is almost more important because of its diminution: one of the eels is a spare brassiere strap. Although the bra on the camel in *Sidewalk* is a significant image, here the bra becomes simply another item in a long list and not the most interesting or noteworthy. Its function is barely worth a titter. In the time between *Attic* and *Falling Up*, sex, sexuality, lingerie, and nudity have declined as subjects of humor, their potential for gaining laughs much diminished. So nudity in this book becomes almost accepted, even full, frontal, *Playboy*-like self-display.

For instance, two women, albeit cartoons, appear naked in this book, one, visible from the rear, prancing in wild abandon, "Dancin' in the Rain" (108) and clearly enjoying it. The other woman, in "Tell Me" (154), is visible from the front but places her hands, in both dejection and embarrassment, over her lower parts; her upper parts are not much detailed. Neither of these illustrations is particularly humorous or titillating, and the women's nudity is not mentioned in their poems at all. In the illustration for "Tattooing Ruth" (45) a naked man is covered with the markings of a suit, but he, too, covers his lower self with his hands, quite naturally and yet quite discreetly. The overall effect of the tattoos is to cover him fully and decently in a double-breasted suit. Never one to detail genitalia, Silverstein judiciously avoids doing so here as well. Although nakedness and sexuality are treated much more casually than in Silverstein's earlier works, the jokes about urination are much broader; in "Gardener" (68), a boy is sent out to water the flowers and is caught as he bends over, back to the reader, to urinate on them. One of the book's bolder jokes is about a person shaped like a helium balloon ("Human Balloon," 125), full of gas from drinking Pepsis and Cokes, a commercial mention rare in this book and elsewhere in Silverstein. As the boy floats about, the narrator of the poem hopes, in an intended pun, that he "doesn't run out of gas." Not mentioned is which end the gas might run out of. Because Silverstein is no longer breaking conventions of decorum and etiquette, which are much more casually observed in poetry and in the popular culture now than earlier, the poems seem much tamer.

Tameness and some human decency are what is remarkable here, especially considering the broad and sometimes bawdy poetry in Silverstein's earlier works. Even parents get their just deserts, with due deference and recognition of the complications and difficulties of their lives. Even in a poem as obviously titled as "No Grown-ups" (113), adults' usefulness becomes clear when the children in the poem find themselves having to pay the bill for pizza at the end. The tacit admission is that grown-ups are really quite handy, and children cannot long get on without them.

The most sympathetic of the poems about adults is "A Cat, a Kid, and a Mom" (104), in which each party complains that it is unfairly persecuted and urged to change, to become something against its nature. This is the first time in all of Silverstein's poems that a parent is a sympathetic figure. The mom explains, "Why try to make me wise?/ . . . Why try to make me be patient and calm? / I'm a *mom*." The mom, whose voice here is authentic and exasperated, simply explains that her behavior is a natural part of parenting, something that can't be changed. The child in the poem gets his own authentic voice—"why try to make me like you?"—and so does the cat. But the mother gets the last word, and her firm foot in the picture, the only part of her shown, suggests the firmness and finality of her voice and her point of view. The mom's insight and the equal standing of her complaint with the child's gives the mom her due, though this poem also admits the child's point of view. Moms are as immutable as cats.

However, adults are not always so sympathetic. The father in "Quality Time" (143) uses his son's nose as a golf tee; although the naive narrator sounds half ironic in his pleasure at spending such rewarding time with the father, the more knowing reader can see through the ruse and realize what most children and adults know: that there is no such thing as quality time without real interaction and that quality time is no panacea for the lack of time a parent spends with a child. Teachers are still not redeemed in this collection, and school is a special focus and target. "Crazy Dream" (168–69) is a potent revenge fantasy during a child's dream in which teachers are forced to answer impossible questions and are swamped with meaningless homework, then hung by their ears from a clothesline for bad behavior.

Silverstein also makes advances in his use of language and of nearly impossible rhymes. "Shanna in the Sauna" (103) practically picks the English language clean of words that rhyme with sauna. "Bituminous?" (134) catalogs the complex, Latinate vocabulary that confuses children. The title suggests one issue—what is the distinction between bituminous and anthracite? between inflammable and incendiary? The fact that this poem rhymes at all shows the poet's growing control over vocabulary and poetry techniques. Some of the poems celebrate peculiarities in the English language. "The Gnome, the Gnat, and the Gnu" (71) celebrates the silent g by using it in improbable places. The gnome, in gnomish English, concludes "[t]hat gnocking a gnat / In the gnoodle like that / Was gnot a gnice thing to do." One of the more hilarious and extended poems describes the trial of "The Nap Taker" (140–41); the child is accused of taking someone else's nap, as if nap taking were somehow related to stealing or kidnapping. Few children take naps willingly, and taking someone else's nap is only a linguistic possibility. The humor is underscored by the accusing judge, who wears a nightcap. The peculiarities of diction are both explored and illustrated in "They Say I Have . . ." (75), about various facial features inherited from other family members: father's nose, for instance. Although the child's behind, his only unique feature, is not shown, ancestors without their inherited features are like a child's puzzle in which the child is asked to draw in hair, eyes, nose, mouth, and so on. Overall, *Falling Up* does not contain the terrible failures found so glaringly, albeit occasionally, in Silverstein's other books; the language is more clearly written for recitation rather than for singing, and the poetry is more technically controlled.

There are fewer poems that preach than in earlier volumes and less celebration of the breaking of rules. But there is still that unalterable faith in the certain knowledge of the individual and in self-direction. *Falling Up* is a book less about changing the world and more about observing its oddities and humor. "The Voice" (38) inside of each person dictates "[w]hat's right for you" without intrusion. This absolute faith in each person's conscience is as iconoclastic as Silverstein gets. This theme, though potently stated here, is not sounded again in the book. There are two poems that comment on the problems of moral paralysis. The diver poised on the diving board who appears at the end of *Attic* reappears here, in "Diving Board" (24), still poised. This kind of procrastination caused by fear is actively discouraged in the poem. Silverstein also counsels courage in "Woulda-Coulda-Shoulda" (65), about three characters who all run away "[f]rom one little *did*." Yet these poems are quieter and more reassuring than those that encourage wild abandon and creativity in the earlier books.

Falling Up ends with a celebration of time, of the problems of living in and for the moment. "The Castle . . ." (171) lies in the land of Now, which is where we all live; the problem is that Now passes so quickly and the castle is only a cardboard facade, so that once someone enters he's automatically deposited out the back of the kingdom and Now has passed. Now is only a moment that passes more quickly than a short poem. This is the poem of someone who knows that many nows have passed and that they are hard to hang on to. This is not the restless spirit at the end of *Sidewalk*, who finds joy in movement and in searching for elusive happiness, nor is it the poet who celebrates human potential in creating the marvelous, as in *Attic*. This is an older, more contented voice that puzzles over the passage of the now without lamenting and is content to contemplate rather than driven to pursue life. The poem facing this one on the left page, "In the Land of . . ." (170), is a celebration of reversals about some other kingdoms. The ideal kingdom is one in which ugly people are held up for public admiration. Some of the reversals are merely overturnings; for instance, in the Kingdom of Listentoemholler, steak is cheap but the tax on it is not. Although this book explores the contradictions and homophones in language particularly effectively, sometimes the logical pursuit of a point gives way to simple if unlikely invention.

Above all, this book succeeds not so much as a tour de force but as a big red bow, tying up some of the issues in Silverstein's productions over the years, showing his increased technical abilities as a poet and his greater concern for the design of a book as a whole. This book is not a bang, not a whimper, but a gentler, kinder book in which some of Silverstein's issues make a playful reappearance and others are resolved. The brashness is gone, which permits the kindness and decency to emerge. If a poet disappears from the publishing scene for 20 years, this is an honorable and excellent way to reappear.

Humor

In all Silverstein books, however, both early and late, it is the humor that sells, convinces, and persuades even the most reluctant readers of poetry. The range of humor in the books makes them appealing to a wide range of school-aged children. It is safe to say that the books are designed for literate children, not for the preliterate. The poems' humor depends on one's ability to read them and interpret the accompanying pictures. An acquaintance with, though not necessarily a love of, the written word and a rudimentary ability to take the cues rendered in the pictures make the poems inaccessible to young children unable to read and interpret the illustrations. The poems also contain a range of humor designed to appeal to children from first to sixth grade and to older children, including adults, who will nostalgically but accurately recall the kinds of humor that most attracted them to Silverstein earlier in their lives.

Though the scholarly investigation of humor is fairly recent and fraught with the difficulty of gaining serious respectability, given the propensity of the subject to take over the tone of the investigation, several scholars have nonetheless developed theories of children's humor and children's acquisition of various senses of humor. Wolfenstein and McGhee are the foremost theorists in the field, the first a Freudian, the second also psychological but more developmental than sexually analytical in approach. In spite of their divergence of perspective, both report, though for differing reasons, basically the same stages in the development of humor in the child.

The first stage, starting at one year old, has less to do with the child producing humorous situations and more to do with the child recognizing contextual clues that indicate that the situation is "just for laughs." Between the ages of two and three, the child sees as humorous the reversals of sex by change of name or ascription of gender.[9] Slightly older children find humor in play with names, especially nicknames, which Wolfenstein finds is particularly offensive to adults, who carry residuals of some ancient, primal instinct about the sacredness of naming.[10] Less mythic analysts may find the same results in similar research, since Americans equate names with personal identity and dignity.

Children at ages four and five think that humor consists of making funny motions and faces. Their linguistic humor is reserved for the contemplation of impossibilities, sometimes linguistically induced possibilities: "Have you ever seen a horse fly?" (as opposed to a horsefly). Such questions do not demand an answer, as a riddle might. In fact, when Wolfenstein sought to teach children of this age riddles, they did not understand the punch lines and saw no humor (pp. 139, 147). Their own versions of funny stories were improbable and shapeless, tending toward no particular end other than an entertaining set of circumstances. For children at this stage and before, Silverstein has little to offer. His target audience has more linguistic sophistication and maturity, as does his humor.

Silverstein begins to appeal to children when they reach age six. At this age, children appear to like joking riddles, both listening to them and telling them. Both Wolfenstein and McGhee report the emergence, like clockwork, among six-year-olds of the "little moron" jokes. Neither reports particularly precocious children learning these rotely memorized jokes early, nor have they found that slow children learn them later. Neither specifies the particular developmental point at which such jokes begin to appear funny to the child or begin to appear as part of the child's repertoire of humor. Wolfenstein, who does point to the consistent themes in the moron jokes of fear of exposure and stupidity (pp. 98, ff.), also reports the jokes' concise verbal quality, which children feel the need to reproduce precisely (pp. 141–44). This is also the stage at which the child is able to control the body long enough to keep it still during the telling of the joke (Wolfenstein, 143); silly gestures are not part of such stories. Wolfenstein also reports the phenomenon that children of this age do not admit to having learned the joke from someone else or to having memorized it; they claim that they have always known it, or that it just exists (pp. 99, 123, 132). For them, jokes are part of the cultural unconscious and simply emerge when the time for telling them is right—this latter is my interpretation of children's sense of the timelessness of such stories.

Concurrent with the appearance of the first moron jokes in children's development, other kinds of joke riddles appear. It is important to note that the child in early grade school is dependent on rote performance of these jokes; the skill of the storyteller, the mood of the audience, the sustaining of the audience's interest are not yet matters of concern (Wolfenstein, 21, 143; Bariaud, 34). But the repertoire of humorous appeal expands, and it is here that Silverstein finds his youngest audience. For the child this age, Silverstein provides joke riddles, such as "What Did?" (*Attic*, 16–17)—"What did the carrot say to the wheat? /'Lettuce' rest, I'm feeling 'beet.' "

Memorizing a Silverstein poem can be a relatively simple experience, since some of the poems are only four lines long. The rhyme and rhythm, as well as the situation's short attenuation until the punch line, help the young reader/reciter remember the poem. Memorizing the poem makes it no longer Silverstein's but the child teller's, a part of that vast lore of childhood that simply is, without authorship. Bathroom humor, the kind that concerns not only feces and urination but also the exposure of the posterior, are prominent features both in children's humor at this stage and in Silverstein's books.

Bathroom humor appears shortly after the child learns control of his bodily functions; their silliness about it often results from the baby-talk words that adults use to describe feces and urine. Older children of reading age still find this subject matter humorous, though they demand more complicated joke forms to relate their amusement in and fascination with this otherwise forbidden topic (Bariaud, 27). Silverstein amply fills this need for jokes and riddles about bathroom behavior and exposure. Although children demand his books and read them, if these volumes ever find their way into the hands of conservative and censorious pedagogues, there will be book-banning attempts. As it stands now, the illicit experience of reading these scatological poems provides fun for children at an age at which the delights of reading and of poetry may still be shrouded in schoolteacher obscurantism. These are not poems for teaching; they are simply to be enjoyed.

Silverstein's poems provide the length, breadth, and variety of jokes to fill most children's need at this age for longer, more complex funny stories. This need stems partly from tensions that children frequently feel during their first years at school; they feel the pressure to achieve, not only from teachers but from parents. The "uproarious" relief that Silverstein's poems provide, if one may borrow a term from the reviewers, and the sheer volume of poems in his collections make the books good resources for stress reduction.

As McGhee points out, as children mature and approach their teens, they are able to tolerate humor in which they are the butt of the joke

(Bariaud, 34). They become storytellers themselves, able to use intonation and timing and to create a mood and develop a story sufficiently to result in a humorous punch line. Silverstein's longer poems lend themselves to such storytelling, especially the tall tales—about being late for school, as in "Kidnapped!" (*Attic*, 159), or about not taking out the garbage, as in "Sara Cynthia Sylvia Stout Would Not Take the Garbage Out" (*Sidewalk*, 70–71); Sara Cynthia is presumably buried by the accumulation she avoids. Older children's willingness to see their own behavior as the source of humor indicates a level of maturity that also signals the end of Silverstein's appeal. Although teenagers report resurrecting old jokes that they might have outgrown (Bariaud, 38), and although adults can similarly regress to the jokes of their childhoods (Wolfenstein, 156), a steady barrage of humor at the level Silverstein presents it does not hold these older readers' attention the same way it does for younger readers. Although adults can be convinced to buy Silverstein's books for children based on their own transitory pleasure in his jokes, children of elementary school age find themselves compelled to read the book repeatedly for yet more entertaining, sustained humor.

Silverstein wisely keeps *Falling Up* from degenerating into a collection of simple school-age jokes by interspersing it with poems that have not only a variety of lengths but also a variety of tones. Unrelenting humor is hard to sustain; Silverstein as a professional cartoonist knew when to change gears. His most consistent, serious concern is promoting the child's powers of creativity and ability to write poetry himself, to amuse himself and others, to think both seriously and humorously. Silverstein's direct, vivid expressions and obvious enjoyment of the same kinds of topics that children find humorous make these encouragements palatable. No teacher here is assigning a poem to be written, no adult is commanding children to enjoy themselves in spite of their own inclinations. The poet is simply a large child himself, capable of perhaps more complex linguistic productions than a child might be but on the other hand a large person still in touch with the smaller person within.

McGhee points to several positive attributes he found consistently among children who were able to produce humor for themselves and others: their language and social skills were more developed than others' their age; they were more energetic; they showed more assertive tendencies in groups; and they showed more concern for, as well as the ability to get for themselves, the positive regard of others (McGhee, 259). A teller of humorous stories of any age knows the pleasure of being the center of attention and of hearing the laughter of listeners. Silverstein knows it too and manages to provide children with the opportunity to get some of this pleasure for themselves.

In terms of the larger scope of American literature for a general readership, Silverstein, who places himself in the tradition of American humor as identified by Jesse Bier in *The Rise and Fall of American Humor,* debunks both by reversal and antiproverbialism.[11] Hamlin Hill claims that there is unlikely to be a single humorist who will speak for the late-twentieth-century United States because of the multiplicity of experiences and voices among its diverse population.[12] Silverstein's works have yet to attain a longevity to merit such a claim for his fame, and two successful volumes rarely constitute a claim to having articulated humor for an entire nation. But it may one day be clear that Silverstein, as the poet of American childhood and as the humorist of American child life, achieved something of that stature for the generations that read his books when they were first published. He stands as a literary predecessor of Jack Prelutsky. By the time today's children become adults and hand Silverstein's books on to their own children and pupils, even Silverstein's toilet jokes may be hallowed.

Notes and References

Chapter One

1. Jean F. Mercier, "Shel Silverstein," *Publishers Weekly* (24 February 1975): 52.
2. Jean Shepard, foreword to Shel Silverstein, *Now Here's My Plan: A Book of Futilities* (New York: Simon and Schuster, 1960), n.p.; hereafter cited in the text as *Futilities*.
3. Perry Nodelman, *Words about Pictures: The Narrative Art of Children's Picture Books* (Athens, Ga.: University of Georgia Press, 1988), 97.
4. Silverstein, "Teevee Jeebies," *Playboy* (July 1959): 77–79.
5. Richard R. Lingeman, "The Third Mr. Silverstein," *New York Times Book Review* (30 April 1978): 57.
6. Silverstein, "The Twenty Commandments," *Playboy* (December 1982): 174–77.
7. Nancy Larrick, "From Tennyson to Silverstein: Poetry for Children, 1910–1985," *Language Arts* 63 (1986): 594.

Chapter Two

1. Silverstein, *The Giving Tree* (New York: Harper and Row, 1964), dust jacket; hereafter cited in the text without page numbers, since there are none in the text.
2. Jacqueline Jackson and Carol Dell, "The Other Giving Tree," *Language Arts* 56, 4 (1979): 427.
3. Barbara Schram, "Misgivings about *The Giving Tree*," *Interracial Books for Children* 5, 5 (1974): 1.
4. Jean Marie Heisberger and Pat McLaughlin, review of *The Giving Tree*, *New Catholic World* 222 (March–April 1979): 92.
5. William Cole, "About Alice, a rabbit, a tree . . . ," *New York Times Book Review* (9 September 1973): 8.
6. Mercier, "Shel Silverstein," 52.
7. Silverstein, *Lafcadio, the Lion Who Shot Back* (New York: Harper and Row, 1963), n.p.; hereafter cited in the text without page numbers, since there are none in the text.
8. Silverstein, *Who Wants a Cheap Rhinoceros?* (1964; revised and expanded, New York: Macmillan, 1983), n.p.
9. Silverstein, *A Giraffe and a Half* (New York: Harper and Row, 1964).

10. Silverstein, *Uncle Shelby's Zoo: Don't Bump the Glump!* (New York: Simon and Schuster, 1964).

11. Silverstein, *Uncle Shelby's ABZ: A Primer for Tender Young Minds* (New York: Simon and Schuster, 1961), n.p.

12. John W. Griffith and Charles H. Frey, eds., *The Classics of Children's Literature* (New York: Macmillan, 1981), 939.

Chapter Three

1. Silverstein, *Where the Sidewalk Ends: The Poems and Drawings of Shel Silverstein* (New York: Harper and Row, 1974), dedication page; hereafter cited in the text as *Sidewalk*.

2. Ursula Nordstrom, "Editing Books for Young People," in *Celebrating Children's Books: Essays on Children's Literature in Honor of Zena Sutherland*, ed. Betsy Hearne and Marilyn Kaye (New York: Lothrop, Lee and Shepard, 1981), 146.

3. "The Worst," for example, first appeared in a slightly different form in *Playboy* (May 1963): 106–9.

4. *The Oxford Book of Children's Verse in America*, ed. Donald Hall (New York: Oxford University Press, 1985).

5. Myra Cohn Livingston, "The Light in His Attic," *New York Times Book Review* (9 March 1986): 36.

6. Robert Browning, "The Pied Piper of Hamelin," in *Story and Verse for Children*, ed. Mildred Blanton Huber (New York: Macmillan, 1940), 193–96.

7. Wally Piper, *The Little Engine That Could*, illustrated by George and Doris Hauman (New York: Platt and Munk, 1930).

8. Livingston, "The Light in His Attic," 37.

9. Alison Lurie, *Don't Tell the Grown-ups: Subversive Children's Literature* (Boston: Little, Brown, 1990), 6.

10. X. J. Kennedy and Dorothy M. Kennedy, "Tradition and Revolt: Recent Poetry for Children," *The Lion and the Unicorn: A Critical Journal of Children's Literature* 4, 2 (1980–81): 75.

11. John Hemphill, "Sharing Poetry with Children: Stevenson to Silverstein," *Advocate* 4 (Fall 1984): 38–44.

12. Edward Blishen, "When I was your age . . .," London *Times Educational Supplement* (23 November 1984): 37.

13. Francine Klagsbrun, ed., *Free to Be . . . You and Me* (New York: McGraw-Hill, 1974); hereafter cited in the text as *Free*.

Chapter Four

1. Silverstein, *A Light in the Attic* (New York: Harper and Row, 1981), 7; hereafter cited in the text as *Attic*.

2. Livingston, "The Light in His Attic," 37.
3. Nodelman, *Words about Pictures*, 119–20.

Chapter Five

1. Joyce Milton, review of *The Missing Piece Meets the Big O*, *New York Times Book Review* (11 October 1981): 39.
2. Silverstein, *The Missing Piece* (New York: Harper and Row, 1976), n.p.; hereafter cited in the text without page numbers, since none are given.
3. Silverstein, *The Missing Piece Meets the Big O* (New York: Harper and Row, 1981), n.p.; hereafter cited in the text without page numbers, since none are given.

Chapter Six

1. Nodelman, *The Pleasures of Children's Literature* (New York: Longman, 1992), 128.
2. Dana Gioia, *Can Poetry Matter? Essays on Poetry and American Culture* (St. Paul, Minn.: Graywolf Press, 1992), 92–93; hereafter cited in the text.
3. Lurie, *Don't Tell the Grown-ups*, 4.
4. Lingeman, "The Third Mr. Silverstein," 57.
5. Nodelman, *The Pleasures*, 11.
6. Kennedy and Kennedy, "Tradition and Revolt" 75.
7. Ann Terry, *Children's Poetry Preferences: A National Survey of Upper Elementary Grades*, NCTE Research Report 16 (Urbana, Ill.: NCTE, 1974), 10–11; Carol J. Fisher and C. Ann Terry, *Children's Language and the Language Arts*, 2nd ed. (New York: McGraw-Hill, 1982), 223.
8. Silverstein, *Falling Up*, poems and drawings by Shel Silverstein (New York, HarperCollins, 1996).
9. Francoise Bariaud, "Age Differences in Children's Humor," in Paul E. McGhee, ed., *Human and Children's Development: A Guide to Practical Applications* (New York: Haworth Press, 1989), 19, 24. Hereafter Bariaud's chapter is cited in the text as Bariaud, McGhee's as McGhee.
10. Martha Wolfenstein, *Children's Humor: A Psychological Approach* (Glencoe, Ill.: The Free Press, 1954), 75; hereafter cited in the text as Wolfenstein.
11. Jesse Bier, "The Rise and Fall of American Humor" (1968), in William Bedford Clark and W. Craig Turner, *Critical Essays on American Humor* (Boston: G. K. Hall, 1984), 105.
12. Hamlin Hill, "The Future of American Humor: Through a Glass Eye, Darkly," in Clark and Turner, *Critical Essays*, 225.

Selected Bibliography

PRIMARY WORKS

Books

Different Dances. New York: Harper, 1979.
Falling Up. New York: HarperCollins, 1996.
A Giraffe and a Half. New York: Harper and Row, 1964.
The Giving Tree. New York: Harper and Row, 1964.
Lafcadio, the Lion Who Shot Back. New York: Harper and Row, 1963.
A Light in the Attic. New York: Harper and Row, 1981.
The Missing Piece. New York: Harper and Row, 1976.
The Missing Piece Meets the Big O. New York: Harper and Row, 1981.
Now Here's My Plan: A Book of Futilities. New York: Simon and Schuster, 1960.
A Playboy's Teevee Jeebies. Chicago: Playboy, 1963.
A Playboy's Teevee Jeebies: Do-It-Yourself Dialogue for the Late Late Show. Chicago: Playboy, 1965.
Uncle Shelby's ABZ: A Primer for Tender Young Minds. New York: Simon and Schuster, 1961.
Uncle Shelby's Zoo: Don't Bump the Glump! New York: Simon and Schuster, 1964.
Where the Sidewalk Ends: The Poems and Drawings of Shel Silverstein. New York: Harper and Row, 1974.
Who Wants a Cheap Rhinoceros? New York: Macmillan, 1964; revised and expanded, New York: Macmillan, 1983.

Albums and Plays

Bobby Bare Sings Lullabys, Legends, and Lies: The Songs of Shel Silverstein. New York: RCA Victor, 1973.
Dirty Feet. Hollis Music, 1968.
Drain My Brain. Cadet, 1968.
Dr. Hook. Columbia, 1972.
Freakin' at the Freakers Ball. Columbia, 1972.
The Great Conch Train Robbery. Columbia, 1980.
The Lady or the Tiger, one-act play produced in New York, 1981.
A Light in the Attic. CBS, 1984.
Ned Kelly. United Artists, 1970.
Sloppy Seconds. Columbia, 1972.
Where the Sidewalk Ends. CBS, 1984.
Who Is Harry Kellerman and Why Is He Saying Those Terrible Things about Me? Columbia, 1971.

SECONDARY SOURCES

Berg-Cross, Linda, and Gary Berg-Cross. "Listening to Stories May Change Children's Social Attitudes." *Reading Teacher* 31 (1978): 659–63. The authors measured kindergartners' attitudes both before and after reading *The Giving Tree* to them and found an increase in their empathy and generosity after the reading.

Campbell, Mary. "Silverstein's Mind Filled with Wandering." *Denver Post Roundup* (30 December 1973): 10. Short interview.

Cole, William. "About Alice, a rabbit, a tree . . ." *New York Times Book Review* (9 September 1973): 8. Admits that the book may be a "male supremacist's fantasy" about the domination of women and the environment. Discusses the book's initial lack of success and then its stardom.

Fisher, Carol J., and Margaret A. Natarella. "Of Cabbages and Kings: Or What Kinds of Poetry Young Children Like." *Language Arts* 56, 4 (April 1979): 380–85. Through a survey, the authors confirmed that children prefer humor and familiar content and form over the obscure and challenging in their poetry.

Hemphill, John. "Sharing Poetry with Children: Stevenson to Silverstein." *Advocate* 4 (Fall 1984): 38–44. The author experiments with an aggressive reading program for elementary school students to introduce them to poetry. At the beginning of the experiment, the only poet's name that the students know is Silverstein's, and at the end of six weeks their favorite poem is "Sick." The author attributes the poem's success to its regular rhythm and rhyme and to its blatant humor.

Jackson, Jacqueline, and Carol Dell. "The Other Giving Tree." *Language Arts* 56, 4 (1979): 427–29. The authors find it difficult to believe that any reader would take the apparent message of *The Giving Tree* seriously.

Kennedy, X. J. "A Rhyme Is a Chime." *New York Times Book Review* (15 November 1981): 51, 60. Praise for Silverstein's authentic voice and outrageous humor from a well-established poet for children. Identifies occasional lapses into sentimentality and vaguely serious feeling as rare flaws.

Kennedy, X. J., and Dorothy M. Kennedy. "Tradition and Revolt: Recent Poetry for Children." *The Lion and the Unicorn: A Critical Journal of Children's Literature* 4, 2 (1980–81): 75–82. Discusses the lack of technical innovation in children's poetry and the tendency of doggerel to masquerade as true poetry for children.

Larrick, Nancy. "From Tennyson to Silverstein: Poetry for Children, 1910–1985." *Language Arts* 63 (1986): 594–600. An overview of tendencies in poetry for children, culminating with Silverstein as a voice of children's genuine experience. Notes that as of the end of April 1986, *Attic* had been on the best-seller list for 164 weeks.

Lingeman, Richard R. "The Third Mr. Silverstein." *New York Times Book Review* (30 April 1978): 57. Discusses Silverstein's avoidance of mythical happy endings and fantasy as a real-life possibility.

Livingston, Myra Cohn. "The Light in His Attic." *New York Times Book Review* (9 March 1986): 36–37. A well-esteemed poet for children deliberately downplays Silverstein's technical flaws in favor of emphasizing his empowerment of children to be creative. Identifies a didactic intent behind the author's humor.

McDowell, Edwin. "Behind the Best Sellers." *New York Times Book Review* (8 November 1981): 50. Discusses the unusual phenomenon of a book of children's poetry reaching the best-seller list.

Mercier, Jean. "Shel Silverstein." *Publishers Weekly* (24 February 1975): 50, 52. A short interview with the author that contains new insights into his personal history and philosophy.

Milton, Joyce. Review of *The Missing Piece Meets the Big O*. *New York Times Book Review* (11 October 1981): 39. Complains that in this book, Silverstein succumbs to being a "publishing phenomenon." Insists that children will not understand the book's meaning.

Nichols, Lewis. "In and Out of Books." *New York Times Book Review* (24 September 1961): 8. Asserts that the success of *ABZ* is due to its treatment of young and old people as human beings like everyone else.

Nordstrom, Ursula. "Editing Books for Young People." In *Celebrating Children's Books: Essays on Children's Literature in Honor of Zena Sutherland*. Ed. Betsy Hearne and Marilyn Kay. New York: Lothrop, Lee and Shepard, 1981. 143–53. Silverstein's editor at Harper and Row comments generally on the difficulties and pleasures of working with authors for young people.

Roiphe, Ann. Review of *The Missing Piece*. *New York Times Book Review* (2 May 1976): 28. Admits that although the story seems aimed at children, its meaning is more likely clearer to "emotionally weary adults."

Schram, Barbara. "Misgivings about *The Giving Tree*." *Interracial Books for Children* 5, 5 (1974): 1, 8. Comments on the themes of dominance and dependence in *Tree*.

Strandburg, Walter L., and Norma J. Livo. "*The Giving Tree*, or There Is a Sucker Born Every Minute." *Children's Literature in Education* 17 (1986): 17–24. Identifies the tree as the "giving mother" and the boy as a "spoiled kid." Finds that few children choose to read the book themselves, preferring to have it read to them by adults unconscious of its alternate messages.

Terry, Ann. *Children's Poetry Preferences*. Urbana, Ill.: National Council of Teachers of English, 1974. Terry's research clearly defines children's likes and dislikes in poetry written for and directed to them; she further suggests different ways of presenting poetry in the classroom so that children will grow to like it.

Index

The Author

Ruth K. MacDonald is college dean for the I Have a Dream Foundation in Hartford, Connecticut. She received her B.A. and M.A. in English from the University of Connecticut, her Ph.D. in English from Rutgers University, and her M.B.A. from the University of Texas at El Paso. She is the author of the volumes on Louisa May Alcott, Beatrix Potter, and Dr. Seuss in Twayne's United States Authors and English Authors Series and of the books *Literature for Children in England and America, 1646–1774* (1982) and *Christian's Children: The Influence of John Bunyan's "Pilgrim's Progress" on American Children's Literature* (1989).